KAREN BROWN'S

English Country Bed & Breakfasts

BOOKS IN KAREN BROWN'S COUNTRY INN SERIES

Austrian Country Inns & Castles

California Country Inns & Itineraries

English Country Bed & Breakfasts

English, Welsh & Scottish Country Inns

European Country Cuisine - Romantic Inns & Recipes

French Country Bed & Breakfasts

French Country Inns & Chateaux

German Country Inns & Castles

Irish Country Inns

Italian Country Inns & Villas

Portuguese Country Inns & Pousadas

Scandinavian Country Inns & Manors

Spanish Country Inns & Paradors

Swiss Country Inns & Chalets

KAREN BROWN'S

English Country Bed & Breakfasts

Written by

June Brown

Sketches by Barbara Tapp

Karen Brown's Country Inn Series

TRAVEL PRESS editors: Karen Brown, Clare Brown, June Brown
Kirsten Price, Iris Sandilands

Technical support: William H. Brown III, Aide-de-camp: William H. Brown
Illustrations: Barbara Tapp
Maps: Cassell Design, Brenden Kootsey
Cover painting: Christina Ladas

This book is written in cooperation with:
Town and Country - Hillsdale Travel
16 East Third Avenue, San Mateo, California 94401

This Warner Books edition is published by arrangement with
Travel Press, San Mateo, California 94401

Warner Books, Inc., 666 Fifth Avenue, New York, NY 10103
A Warner Communications Company

Printed in the United States of America
First Warner Books Trade Paperback Printing: April 1991
10 9 8 7 6 5 4 3 2 1

LIBRARY OF CONGRESS

Library of Congress Cataloging-in-Publication Data

Brown, June, 1949-
Karen Brown's English country bed & breakfasts / written by June Brown : sketches by Barbara Tapp.
p. cm. -- (Karen Brown's country inn series)
Includes index.
ISBN 0-446-39280-4
1. Bed and breakfast accommodations--England--Guide-books.
2. England--Description and travel--1971---Guide-books. I. Brown, Karen. II. Title. III. Title: English country bed and breakfasts. IV. Title: English country bed and breakfasts. V. Series
TX907.5.G72E5433 1991
647.94203--dc20

90-12869
CIP

For My Family

Contents

Introduction

From the charm of a thatched cottage down a leafy lane to the grandeur of an ancestral manor this guide offers you the opportunity to enjoy the special ambiance of such homes. Interspersed with these idyllic places are traditional pubs and welcoming guest houses that offer wholehearted hospitality in charming surroundings. Every place to stay that is included in this guide is one that we have seen and enjoyed - our personal recomendation written with the sincere belief that where you lay your head each night makes the difference between a good and a great vacation. We encourage you to buy new editions of our guides and throw away old ones--you will be glad you did because we add new listings, update prices, phone and fax numbers and delete places that have not maintained standards.

ABOUT BED AND BREAKFAST TRAVEL

Every inclusion in this book has a different approach to bed and breakfast. Some households are very informal, some welcome children, and others invite you to sample gracious living--cocktails in the drawing room, billiards after dinner, and croquet on the lawn. The one thing that they have in common is a warmth of welcome. We have tried to be candid and honest in our appraisals and tried to convey each listing's special flavor so that you know what to expect and will not be disappointed. To help you appreciate and understand what to expect when staying at listings in this guide the following pointers are given in alphabetical order, not order of importance.

Animals: Even if animals are not mentioned in the write-up, the chances are that there are friendly, tail-wagging dogs and sleek cats as visible members of the families.

Arrival and Departure: Always discuss your time of arrival--hosts usually expect you to arrive around 6:00 pm. If you are going to arrive late or early, be certain to telephone your host. You are expected to leave by 10:00 am on the morning of your departure. By and large you are not expected to be on the premises during the day.

Bathrooms: Stating that a bedroom has a *private* bathroom indicates that the bathroom is for the exclusive use of one bedroom and it may be down the hall or ensuite in the room.

Bedrooms: Beds are often made with duvets (down comforters) versus the more traditional blankets and sheets. A double room has one double bed, a twin room has two single beds, and a family room contains one or more single beds in addition to a double bed. American king and queen beds are few and far between.

Children: Places that welcome children state *Children welcome*. The majority of listings in this guide do not "welcome" children but find they become tolerable at different ages over 5 or, more often than not, over 12. In some cases places simply do not accept children and the listing states *No children*. However, these indications of children's acceptability are not cast in stone, so if you have your heart set on staying at a listing that states *children over 12* and you have an 8-year-old, call them, explain your situation, and they may well accept you. Ideally we would like to see all listings welcoming children and all parents remembering that they are staying in a home and doing their bit by making sure that children do not run wild. A list of places that "welcome" children of any age is given on pages 139 and 140.

Christmas: Several listings offer Christmas getaways--if the information section indicates that the listing is open during the Christmas season there is a very good chance that it offers a festive Christmas package.

Credit Cards: The majority of places in this guide do not accept plastic payment. Whether accommodation accepts payment by credit card is indicated using the terms *AX* - American Express, *MC* - Master Card, *VS* - Visa or simply *all major*.

Directions: We give concise driving directions to guide you to the listing which is often in a more out-of-the-way place than the town or village in the address. We would be very grateful if you would let us know of cases where our directions have proved inadequate.

Electricity: The voltage is 240. Most bathrooms have razor points (American style) for 110 volts. If you are coming from overseas it is recommended that you take only dual voltage appliances and a kit of electrical plugs. Often your host can loan you a hairdryer and an iron.

Maps: Each Place to Stay is referenced to one of the maps on pages 13 to 19 showing the location of the town or village nearest the lodging. These are an artist's renderings and are not intended to replace commercial maps. Our suggestion is to purchase a large-scale road atlas of England where an inch equals 10 miles.

Meals: Prices quoted always include breakfast. Breakfast is most likely to be juice, a choice of porridge or cereal, followed by a plate of egg, bacon, sausage, tomatoes, and mushrooms completed by toast, marmalade, and jams. A great many places offer evening meals which should be requested at the time you make your reservation. You cannot expect to arrive at a bed and breakfast and receive dinner if you have not made reservations several days in advance. At some homes the social occasion of guests and host gathered around the dining room table for an evening dinner party is a large part of the overall experience--many of these types of listings expect their guests to dine in. Places that do not offer evening meals are always happy to make recommendations for guests at nearby pubs or restaurants.

Rates: Rates are those quoted to us for the 1991 summer season. We have tried to standardize rates by quoting the 1991 per person bed and breakfast rate based on two people occupying a room. Not all places conform so where dinner is included, or the listing only quotes the double rate we have stated this in the listing. Prices are always quoted to include breakfast, Value Added Tax (VAT), and service (if these are applicable). Please use the figures printed as a guideline and be certain to ask what the rate is at the time of booking. Prices for a single are usually higher than the per person rates and prices for a family room are sometimes lower. Many listings offer special terms, below their normal prices, for "short breaks" of two or more nights. In several listings suites are available at higher prices.

Reservations: Reservations can be confining and usually must be guaranteed by a deposit; however, if you have your heart set on a particular place, to avoid disappointment make a reservation. If you prefer to travel as whim and the weather dictate, rooms can often be had in the countryside with just a few days' notice. July and August are the busiest times and if you are travelling to a popular spot such as Bath or York it is advisable to make reservations.

It is completely unacceptable practice to make reservations for a particular night at several establishments choosing at the last minute which one to stay at.

Although proprietors do not always strictly adhere to it, it is important to understand that once reservations are confirmed--whether by phone or in writing--you are under contract. This means that the proprietor is legally obligated to provide the accommodation he has promised and that you are bound to pay for that accommodation. If you cannot take up your accommodation, you are liable for a portion of the accommodation charges plus your deposit. If you have to cancel your reservation, do so as soon as possible so that the proprietor can attempt to re-let your room--in which case you are liable only for the re-let fee or the deposit.

If you are visiting from overseas, our preference for making a reservation is by telephone; the cost is minimal and you have your answer immediately, so if space is not available you can then decide on an alternate. (If calling from the United States allow for the time difference [England is five hours ahead of New York] so that you can call during their business day. Dial 011 [the international code], 44 [Britain's code], then the city code (dropping the 0) and the telephone number.) Be specific as to what your needs are, such as a ground-floor room, ensuite bathroom or twin beds. Check the prices which may well have changed from those given in the book (summer 1991). Ask what deposit to send or give your credit card number. Tell them about what time you intend to arrive and request dinner if you want it. Ask for a confirmation letter with brochure and map to be sent to you.

Sightseeing: We have tried to mention major sightseeing attractions near each lodging to encourage you to spend several nights in each location. Few countries have as much to offer as England--within a few miles of every listing there are places of interest to visit and explore--lofty cathedrals, quaint churches, museums, and grand country houses.

Smoking: Nearly all listings forbid smoking either in the bedrooms or public rooms. Some allow no smoking at all, in which case we state *No Smoking house* as the second to last line of the listing. A list of no smoking houses is on page 141. Ask about smoking policies if this is important to you--best to be forewarned rather than frustrated.

Socializing: We have tried to indicate the degree of socializing that is included in your stay as some hosts treat their guests like visiting friends and relatives, sharing cocktails, eating with them around the dining room table, and joining them for coffee after dinner (the difference being that friends and relatives do not receive a bill at the end of their stay).

Wolsey Lodges: Several of the listings are members of Wolsey Lodges, a consortium of private houses that open their doors to a handful of guests at a time. Visitors become a part of the household--guests are not expected to scuttle up to their rooms and family life does not carry on away from guests behind closed doors. As with all the listings in this guide, Wolsey Lodge members approach bed and breakfast in different ways--some are informal, while others offer a taste of refined, gracious living. If a lodging is a member of this group, we state *Wolsey Lodge* in the information section. A color brochure listing all the Wolsey Lodge properties is available from Wolsey Lodges, 17 Chapel Street, Bildeston, Suffolk IP7 7EP, tel: 0449 741297, fax 0449 741590. Places in this guide that are members of Wolsey Lodges are listed on pages 142 and 143.

FACTS ABOUT ENGLAND

Driving: Just about the time overseas visitors board their return flight home they will have adjusted to driving on the "right" side which is the left side in England. You must contend with such things as roundabouts (circular intersections); flyovers (overpasses); ring roads (peripheral roads whose purpose is to bypass city traffic); lorries (trucks); lay-bys (turn-outs); boots (trunks) and bonnets (hoods). Pedestrians are permitted to cross the road anywhere and always have the right of way. Seat belts must be worn at all times

Motorways: The letter "M" precedes these convenient ways to cover long distances. With three lanes of traffic either side of a central divider you should stay in the left-hand lane except for passing. Motorway exits are numbered and correspond to numbering on major road maps. Service areas supply petrol, cafeterias, and "bathrooms" (the word "bathroom" is used in the American sense--in Britain "bathroom" means a room with a shower or bathtub, not a toilet--"loo" is the most commonly used term for an American bathroom).

"A" Roads: The letter "A" precedes the road number. All major roads fall into this category. They vary from three lanes either side of a dividing barrier to single carriageways with an unbroken white line in the middle indicating that passing is not permitted. These roads have the rather alarming habit of changing from dual to single carriageway at a moment's notice.

"B" Roads and Country Roads: The letter "B" preceding the road number or the lack of any lettering or numbering indicate that it belongs to the maze of country roads that crisscross Britain. These are the roads for people who have the luxury of time to enjoy the scenery enroute. Arm yourself with a good map (although getting lost is part of the adventure). Driving these narrow roads is terrifying at first but exhilarating after a while. Meandering down these roads, you can expect to spend time crawling behind a tractor or cows being herded to the farmyard. Some lanes are so narrow that there is room for only one car.

Information: The British Tourist Authority is an invaluable source of information. Offices are located in the United States and Canada at:

ATLANTA: The British Tourist Authority, #470, 2580 Cumberland Parkway, Atlanta, GA 30339, tel (404) 432 9635

CHICAGO: The British Tourist Authority, #1510, 625 North Michigan Ave., Chicago, IL 60611, tel (312) 787 0490

LOS ANGELES: The British Tourist Authority, World Trade Center, 350 South Figueroa St., Suite 450, Los Angeles, CA 90071, tel (213) 628 3525

NEW YORK: The British Tourist Authority, 40 West 57th Street, 3rd floor, New York, NY 10019, tel (212) 581 4700

TORONTO: The British Tourist Authority, 94 Cumberland Street, Suite 600, Toronto, Ontario M5R 3N3, tel (416) 961 8124

If you need additional information while you are in Britain there are more than 700 official Tourist Information Centres identified by a blue and white letter "i" and "Tourist Information." In London the British Travel Centre at 4-12 Lower Regent Street, London SW1 (near Piccadilly Circus tube station) provides information on what to see and do, and how to do it, all year round in Britain. There are an American Express travel service office, a bureau de change, and a British Rail ticket office there, so you can book a room, buy air or train tickets, hire a car or pay for a coach tour or theater tickets in one location. The Centre also has changing exhibitions put on by the National and Regional Tourist Boards, and a "video wall" where several screens display films of attractions to be found round the country. The Centre is open seven days a week, 9:00 am to 6:30 pm Monday to Saturday, 10:00 am to 4:00 pm on Sunday.

Pubs: Pubs are a British institution. Traditional pubs with inviting names such as the Red Lion, Wheatsheaf, and Kings Arms are found at the heart of every village. Not only are they a great place to meet the locals over a pint or a game of dominoes or darts, but they offer an inviting place to dine. Meals served in the bar enable you to enjoy an inexpensive meal while sipping your drink in convivial surroundings. Bar meals range from a bowl of soup to an inviting cooked dinner. Many pubs have dining rooms that serve more elaborate fare in equally convivial but more sophisticated surroundings. The key to success when dining at a pub is to obtain a recommendation from where you are staying that night--your host or hostess is always happy to assist you.

Shopping: Overseas visitors can reclaim the 15% VAT (Value Added Tax) that they pay on the goods they purchase. Not all stores participate in the refund scheme and there is often a minimum purchase price. Stores that do participate will ask to see your passport before completing the VAT form. This form must be presented with the goods to the Customs officer at the point of departure from Britain within three months of purchase. The customs officer will certify the form which you return to the store where you bought the goods. The store will then send you a check in sterling for the refund.

Weather: Britain has a tendency to be moist at all times of the year. The cold in winter is rarely severe; however, the farther north you go the greater the possibility of being snowed in. Spring can be wet but it is a lovely time to travel; the summer crowds have not descended, daffodils and bluebells fill the woodlands, and the hedgerows are filled with wildflowers. Summer offers the best chance of sunshine but also the largest crowds. Schools are usually closed the last two weeks of July and all of August--this is the time when most families take their summer holidays. Travel is especially hectic on the weekends in summer--try to avoid major routes and airports at these times. Autumn is also an ideal touring time. The weather tends to be drier than in spring and the woodlands are decked in their golden autumn finery.

Key Map

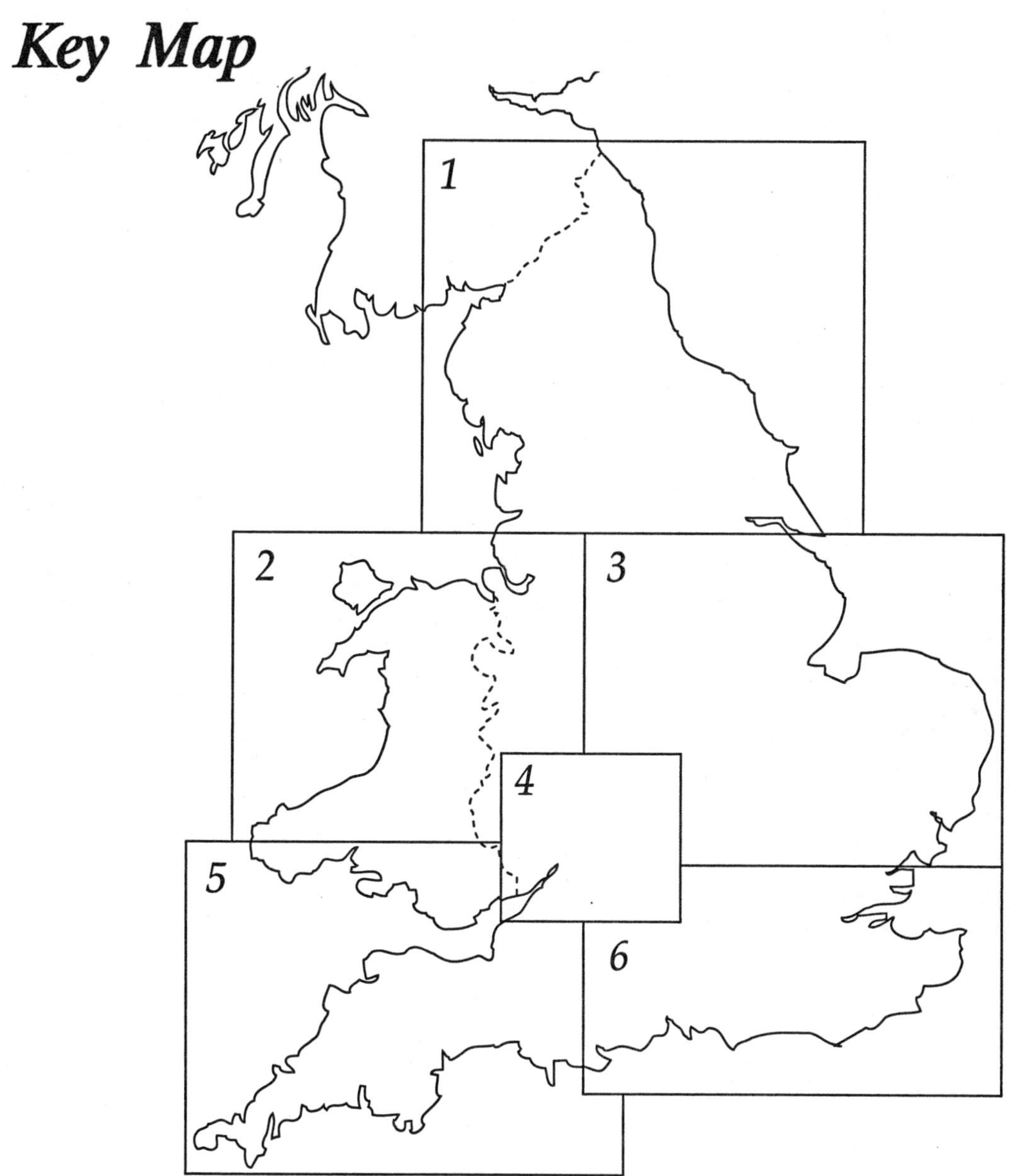

Map 1

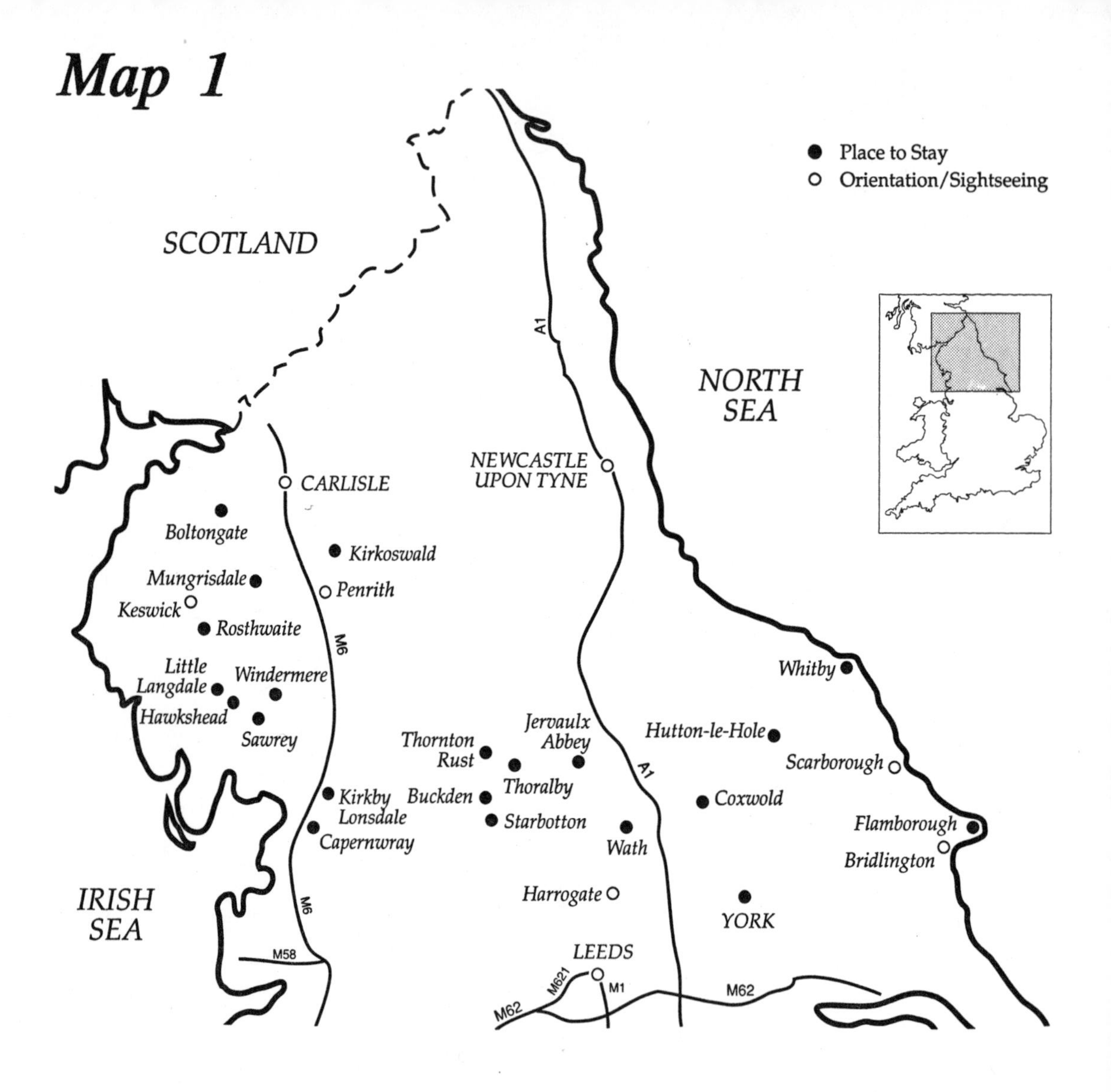

Place to Stay
Orientation/Sightseeing
SCOTLAND
NORTH SEA
IRISH SEA
CARLISLE
NEWCASTLE UPON TYNE
A1
M6
M58
M62
M621
M1
Boltongate
Kirkoswald
Mungrisdale
Penrith
Keswick
Rosthwaite
Little Langdale
Windermere
Hawkshead
Sawrey
Thornton Rust
Thoralby
Jervaulx Abbey
Buckden
Starbotton
Kirkby Lonsdale
Capernwray
Wath
Harrogate
LEEDS
YORK
Coxwold
Hutton-le-Hole
Whitby
Scarborough
Flamborough
Bridlington

Map 2

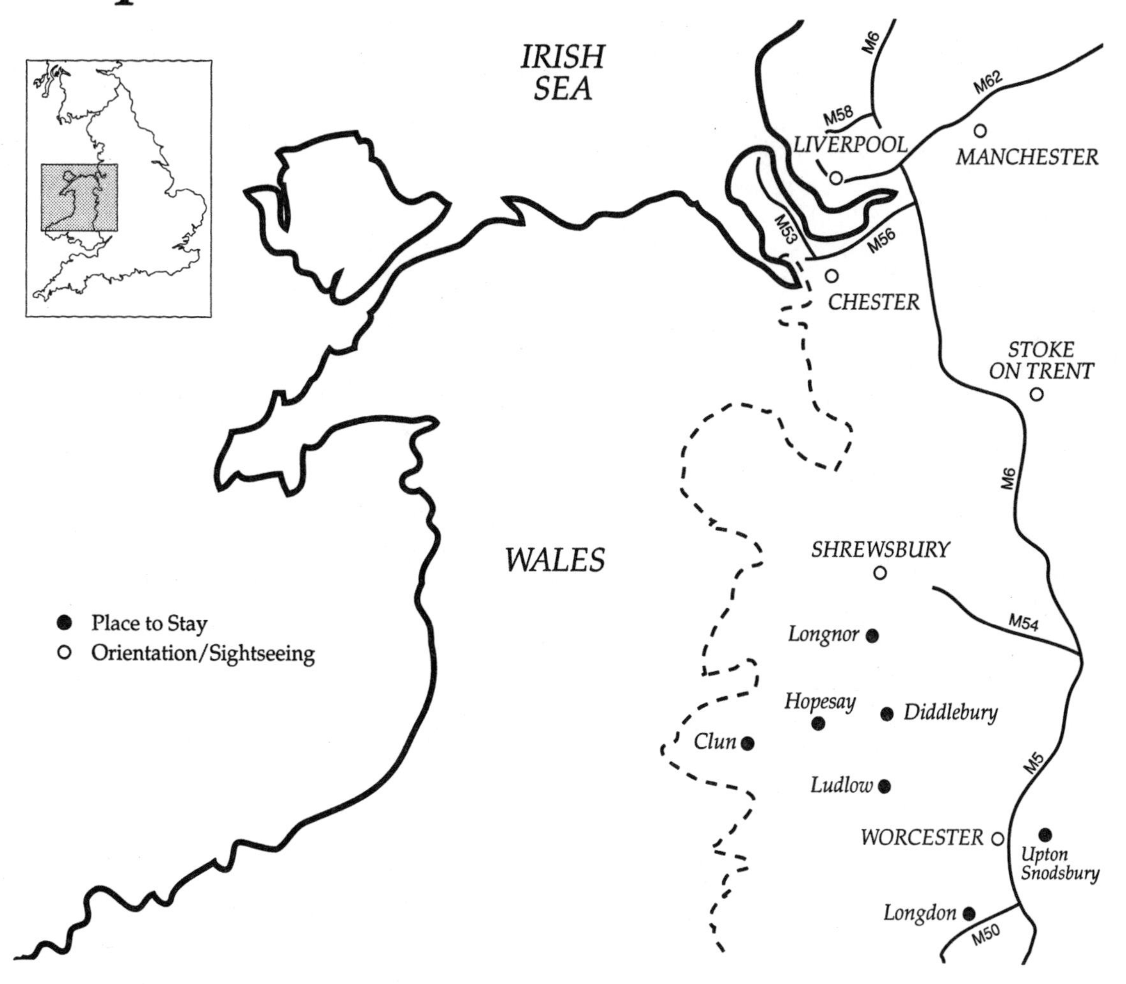
IRISH SEA
WALES
M6
M62
M58
LIVERPOOL
MANCHESTER
M53
M56
CHESTER
STOKE ON TRENT
M6
SHREWSBURY
M54
Longnor
Hopesay
Diddlebury
Clun
Ludlow
M5
WORCESTER
Upton Snodsbury
Longdon
M50
Place to Stay
Orientation/Sightseeing

Map 3

M1
A1
M18
SHEFFIELD
Babworth
Hathersage
Rowland
Lincoln
Bakewell
Leek
Wetton
Bottom House
Blore
Ashbourne
M1
NOTTINGHAM
Bourne
LEICESTER
A1
BIRMINGHAM
M69
Hallaton
M6
COVENTRY
Warwick
NORTHAMPTON
Stratford
upon Avon
M1
Olney
OXFORD
Place to Stay
Orientation/Sightseeing
Cley next the Sea
King's Lynn
W. Lexham
NORWICH
Northwold
Long Stratton
Fersfield
Saxmundham
Tannington
Saxtead Green
CAMBRIDGE
Otley
Needham Market
Stoke by
Nayland
IPSWICH
Ickleton
Dedham
Castle
Hedingham
Higham
M11
Colchester
NORTH
SEA

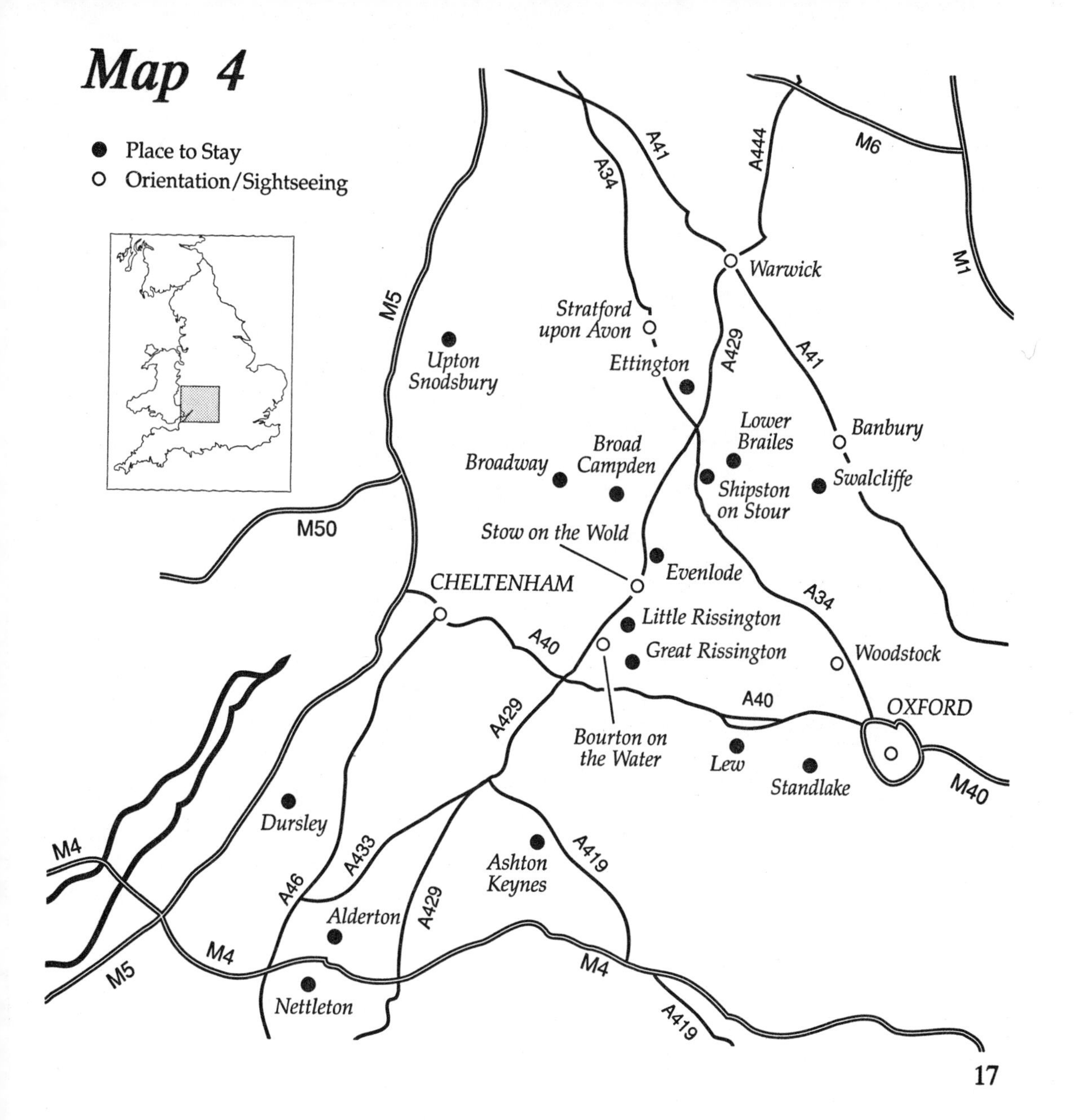
Map 4
Place to Stay
Orientation/Sightseeing
M5
M6
M1
M50
M4
M40
A41
A34
A444
A429
A40
A433
A46
A419
Warwick
Stratford upon Avon
Ettington
Upton Snodsbury
Lower Brailes
Banbury
Broadway
Broad Campden
Shipston on Stour
Swalcliffe
Stow on the Wold
Evenlode
CHELTENHAM
Little Rissington
Great Rissington
Woodstock
OXFORD
Bourton on the Water
Lew
Standlake
Dursley
Ashton Keynes
Alderton
Nettleton

Map 5

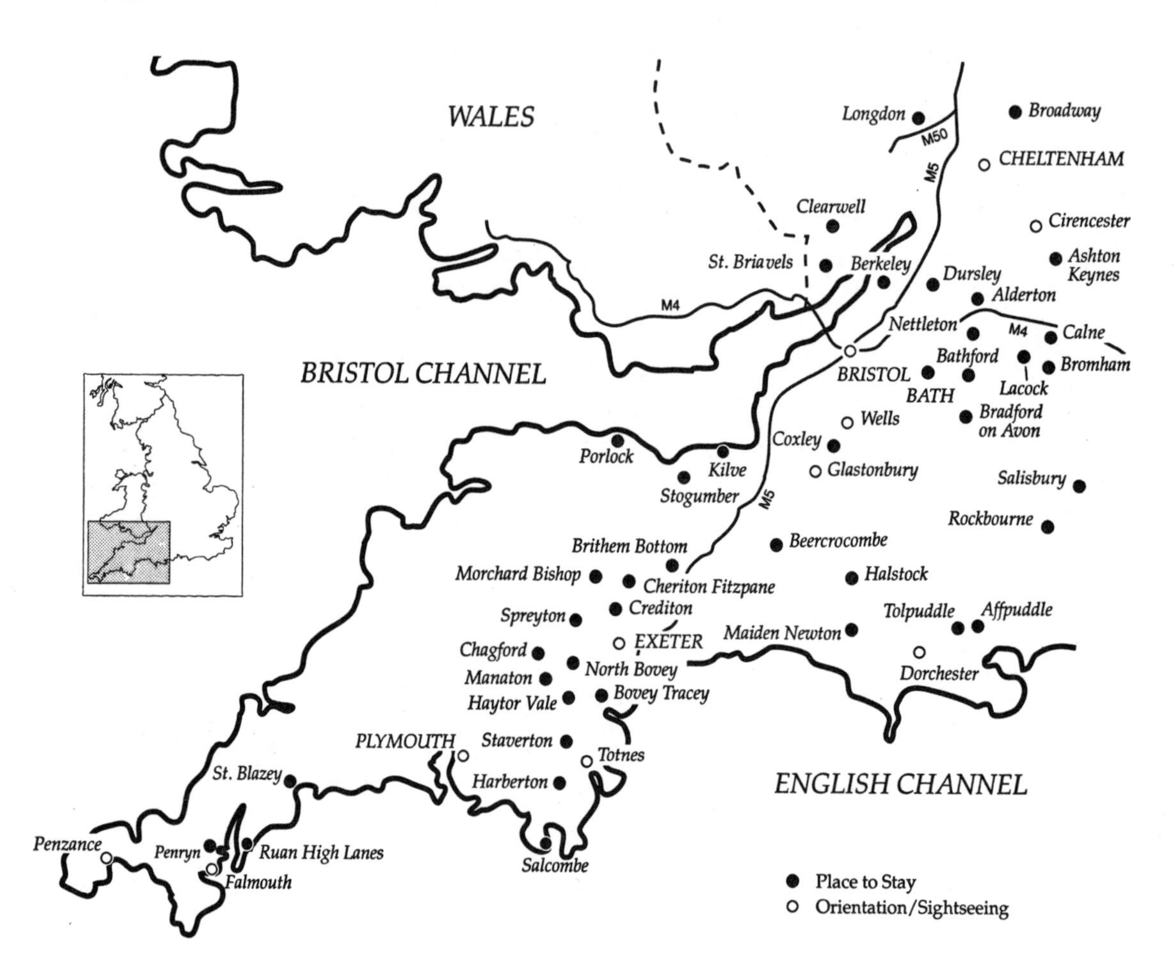

WALES
BRISTOL CHANNEL
ENGLISH CHANNEL
Longdon
Broadway
M50
M5
CHELTENHAM
Clearwell
Cirencester
St. Briavels
Berkeley
Ashton Keynes
Dursley
Alderton
M4
Nettleton
Calne
BRISTOL
Bathford
Bromham
BATH
Lacock
Wells
Bradford on Avon
Coxley
Porlock
Kilve
Glastonbury
Salisbury
Stogumber
Rockbourne
Beercrocombe
Brithem Bottom
Halstock
Morchard Bishop
Cheriton Fitzpane
Crediton
Tolpuddle
Affpuddle
Spreyton
Maiden Newton
EXETER
Chagford
North Bovey
Dorchester
Manaton
Haytor Vale
Bovey Tracey
PLYMOUTH
Staverton
Totnes
St. Blazey
Harberton
Penzance
Penryn
Ruan High Lanes
Salcombe
Falmouth
Place to Stay
Orientation/Sightseeing

Map 6

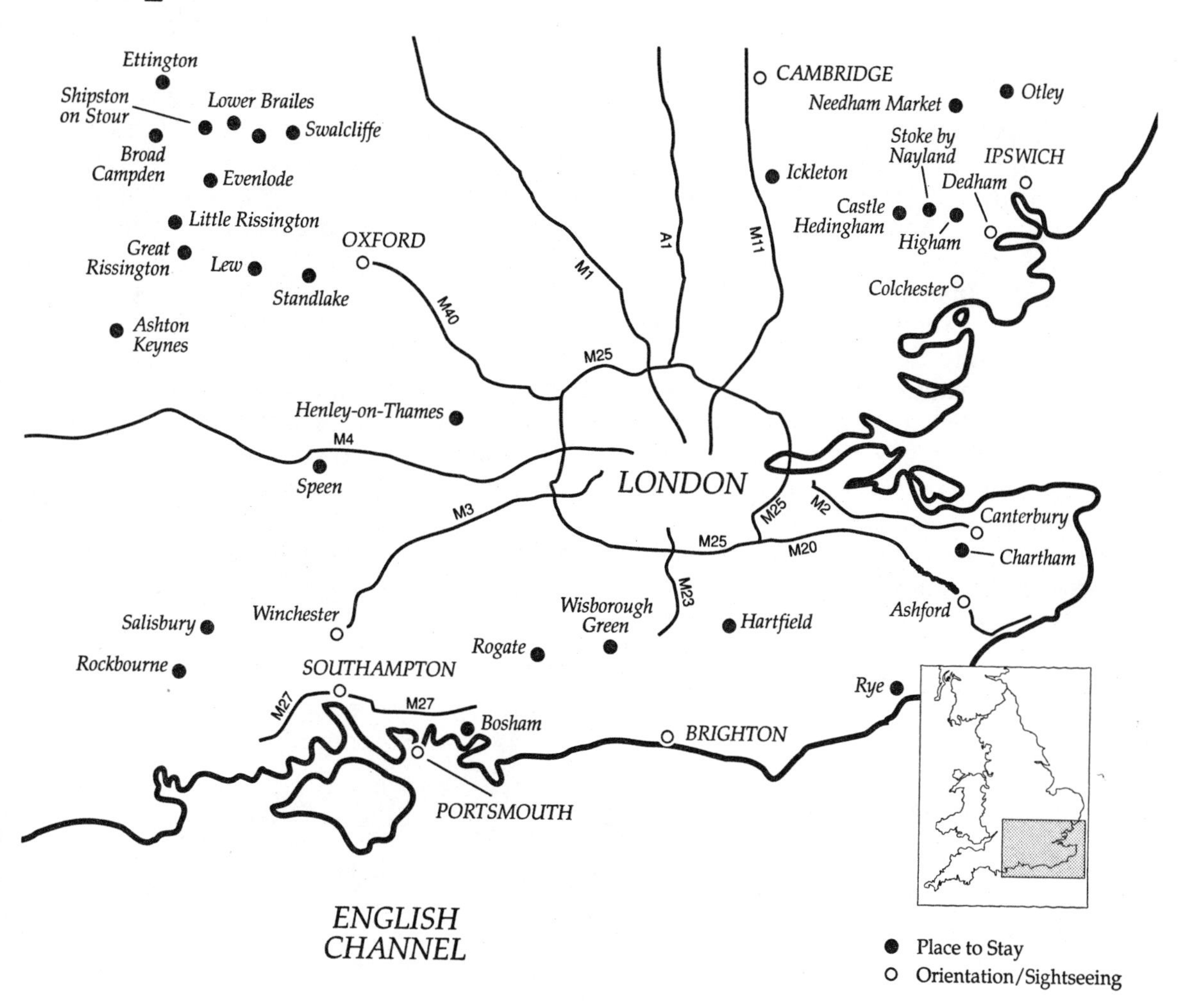

Ettington
Shipston on Stour
Lower Brailes
Swalcliffe
Broad Campden
Evenlode
Little Rissington
Great Rissington
Lew
Standlake
OXFORD
Ashton Keynes
M40
M1
A1
M11
CAMBRIDGE
Needham Market
Otley
Stoke by Nayland
IPSWICH
Ickleton
Dedham
Castle Hedingham
Higham
Colchester
M25
Henley-on-Thames
M4
Speen
LONDON
M3
M25
M2
Canterbury
M25
M20
Chartham
M23
Wisborough Green
Hartfield
Ashford
Salisbury
Winchester
Rogate
Rockbourne
SOUTHAMPTON
Rye
M27
M27
Bosham
BRIGHTON
PORTSMOUTH
ENGLISH CHANNEL
Place to Stay
Orientation/Sightseeing

The Old Vicarage offers visitors an exceptionally delightful place to stay in this tranquil part of the country immortalized in Thomas Hardy's novels. Standing next to the old village church, surrounded by green lawns, neatly clipped hedges, and rose gardens, this fine Georgian house is owned by the warmly gracious Anthea and Michael Hipwell who have lovingly furnished all the rooms with beautiful antiques and objets d'art. Nothing is stiffly formal (as the British would say, "over the top"). Instead, the ambience is one of refined elegance such as you would experience in the loveliest English manor. Breakfast is the only meal that Anthea prepares, but she has a long list of wonderful restaurants in the surrounding villages. Upstairs the bedrooms have pretty wallpapers and are furnished in tasteful English country style, in character with the decor throughout The Old Vicarage. There is a lot to see and do in the area: Cerne Abbas with its thatched cottage and giant carved into the hillside is the Casterbridge of Hardy's novels, and historic Dorchester, Salisbury, and Shaftesbury are nearby. *Directions:* From Dorchester take the A35 northeast for 5 miles to Tolpuddle (this is the village where the six martyrs met to fight starvation farmworkers' wages) where you turn left for Affpuddle (1 mile).

THE OLD VICARAGE
Owners Michael & Anthea Hipwell
Affpuddle
Dorchester, Dorset DT2 7HH
Tel: (0305) 848315
3 rooms, 1 with private bathroom
From £17.50 per person
Open all year
Children over 12

True to its name, Manor Farm is very much a working farm, growing barley and wheat and raising cattle for beef. Guests are welcome to wander round the grounds, watch the children ride ponies in the paddock, and explore the farmyard. For the inquisitive, Jeffrey is happy to give a conducted tour of the property. Victoria is helped in the house by Jenny who keeps everything immaculate and is always on hand to welcome guests. All the rooms of this large gabled farmhouse are furnished with an informal mixture of antique and more modern furniture. From the plump, flowered sitting room sofa you can enjoy a blazing fire in the huge fireplace or simply relax watching the television in this comfortable room. Breakfast is the only meal served in the dining room; for other meals guests often eat at the pub in nearby Luckington. The large double room overlooking the farmyard has an ensuite bathroom and at the time of my visit plans were well under way to add bathrooms to each of the additional two bedrooms. Alderton lies at the southern edge of the Cotswolds--very rural, yet well placed to visit Bath, Bristol, Malmesbury, and Tetbury. Every May the Badminton horse trials are held nearby. *Directions:* Leave the M4 at junction 17, following signs for Malmesbury. Take the first left, B4040, through Stanton to Grittleton, then turn right at the crossroads for Alderton where Manor Farm faces the church.

MANOR FARM
Owners Victoria & Jeffrey Lippiat
Alderton
Chippenham, Wiltshire SN14 6NL
Tel: (0666) 840271
3 rooms with private bathrooms
From £20 per person
Open March to November
Children over 12

Whenever Peter or Elizabeth Hartland see people peering curiously up their driveway they know they're Richmonds looking for their "roots," for Cove House was the home of John Richmond who went with the men of Taunton to found Taunton, Massachusetts in 1640 and the Richmonds belong to the Richmond Society, a group who can trace their ancestors back to this wisteria-festooned cottage. Guests enjoy breakfast in the gracious dining room where lovely flower arrangements dress antique furniture. The bedrooms are large and some can take an extra child's bed and cot. In the small adjacent study, an alcove lined with a detailed map of the area illustrates the many places of interest round and about: Avebury, Blenheim Palace, Oxford, Bath, and the Cotswold villages. Nearby, flooded gravel pits which attract many species of waterfowl provide a birdwatcher's paradise. Peter, a retired schoolmaster, keeps informational brochures on hand for visitors' use and has also compiled a "good food guide" to local pubs and restaurants. Guests often walk the short distance into the village to eat at the White Hart or the Horse and Jockey. With advance notice Elizabeth is happy to prepare an evening meal for guests. *Directions:* The village of Ashton Keynes is 6 miles south of Cirencester. In the center of the village is the White Hart--100 yards east a large wall bounds the driveway. Drive through the inner gate.

COVE HOUSE
Owners Major Peter & Elizabeth Hartland
2 Cove House
Ashton Keynes, Wiltshire SN6 6NS
Tel: (0285) 861221
4 rooms with private bathrooms
From £17 per person
Closed December & January
Children welcome
Wolsey Lodge

The Barns is a comfortable spot to break a long journey between London and Edinburgh via the A1, or for a longer visit to explore Nottinghamshire. This county is famous not only for the exploits of Robin Hood, but also as the area where the Pilgrim Fathers formed their separatist church before setting sail for America and establishing a new colony. The Barns is the very tastefully converted hay and tractor barns of the next-door farm, and behind its red brick facade all is spick and span. A sofa and chairs are drawn around a crackling log fire, and tables are topped with linen cloths neatly laid for breakfast. With advance notice Rosalie is happy to cook a traditional roast dinner. Upstairs the bedrooms are plainly decorated with cream walls highlighting dark beams and all have nice touches such as a fresh posy of flowers on a small antique dresser and elegant china tea cups. Room 1 is a particularly large family suite. A pleasant drive through Sherwood Forest brings visitors to the Visitor Centre which has an exhibition on Robin Hood and his merry band and offers maps guiding you through ancient oaks trees to his former hideaways. Clumber Park near Sherwood Forest is noted for its main driveway planted with over 1,296 lime trees. *Directions:* From the south take the A1 north to the A57 (Worksop) roundabout, make a U turn and go south on the A1. Take the first left, on the B6420, towards Retford. The Barns is on the left.

THE BARNS
Owner Rosalie Brammer
Morton Farm, Babworth
Retford, Nottinghamshire DN22 8HA
Tel: (0777) 706336
6 rooms with private bathrooms
From £18 per person
Closed Christmas
Credit cards VS
Children welcome

Bath ranks as one of Britain's most important Roman sites and one of its most visited cities outside of London. Situated halfway up a steep hill, Somerset House is a classic Regency abode of warm, honey-colored stone, set in a spacious garden affording panoramic views of the city. The family pets along with family photos and books give a comfortable feeling to Jean and Malcolm Seymour's upscale guest house. Son Jonathan is the chef and his traditional English cuisine includes many regional specialties. The basement dining room is decorated with country flair, featuring light wood Windsor chairs, lace-topped tables, and a huge pine dresser set upon the checkerboard tile floor. The guest bedrooms, named after the sons and daughters of George III, have a light, airy feeling complemented by matching drapes and bedspreads and whimsical rag dolls propped up on the pillows. Several rooms have an extra bed and a ground floor room is ideal for those who have difficulty with stairs. All have a coffee and tea tray, radio, and telephone. There is no television. A fifteen-minute walk brings you into the heart of Bath: the abbey, the Pump Room and Roman baths, the streets and squares lined with Georgian houses, the shopping arcades, and much else. *Directions:* Do not go into the city center, but follow signs for the University. Going up Bathwick Hill, Somerset House is on the corner of the third turning to the left.

SOMERSET HOUSE
Owners Jean & Malcolm Seymour
35 Bathwick Hill
Bath, Avon BA2 6LD
Tel: (0225) 466451/463471
9 rooms with private bathrooms
From £27.50 per person
Open all year
Children over 10
No Smoking house

This listed Georgian country house is one of the many lovely homes in the conservation village of Bathford. The Orchard is set in its own walled grounds which feature sweeping lawns and a magnificent variety of old trees. It is difficult to believe that the bustling city of Bath is just 15 minutes away from this tranquil spot. John and Olga London have a winning formula of a handsome house in beautiful surroundings, immaculately decorated and furnished with a tasteful mixture of fine antiques. Guests have full use of a very elegant yet very welcoming sitting room where a log fire blazes on chilly evenings and high French doors and a large window open up to views of the perfectly groomed garden. Upstairs are three very generously proportioned, high-ceilinged bedrooms with large bay windows, discreetly placed televisions, and spacious bathrooms. The two front bedrooms have enviable views of an enormous copper beech tree, reputedly over 200 years old, and across the valley to green fields. The fourth bedroom, nicknamed "The Folly," has a private garden entrance, lower ceilings, and small windows that overlook the garden. Guests who enjoy a country walk are directed across the orchard to a 600-acre nature reserve. Most guests stroll down the hill to dine at The Crown Inn. *Directions:* Leave the M4 at junction 18 and follow the A46 south to the A4 (towards Chippenham), turn right onto the A363 and left, at The Crown Inn, into Bathford. The Orchard is halfway up the hill on the right.

THE ORCHARD
Owners John & Olga London
Bathford
Bath, Avon BA1 7TG
Tel: (0225) 858765
4 rooms with private bathrooms
From £55 double
Open March to October
Children over 12

Frog Street Farm, a lovely gray, stone farmhouse dating back to 1436, is a real working farm where things are not fancy or cutesy pretty, but everything fits together perfectly with country freshness. From the moment you are met at the door by Veronica, with her true country-style warmth and jolly sense of humor, the mood is set. You are immediately made to feel part of the family and offered a cup of tea in front of the large inglenook fireplace before being shown to your room. The guest rooms are spotlessly clean and simply, but prettily, decorated with a color scheme of pinks and greens used throughout the house. The front garden is ablaze with color in the summer. Just across the road from the farmhouse there is a swimming pool set in an open field. Veronica takes great pride in her cooking and, with advance notice, will prepare delicious meals from farm-fresh produce. For those who want to spend a few days in the country, away from city sophistication, Frog Street Farm is the epitome of what a farm vacation should be. In this pretty, rolling countryside are the charming little towns of Chard, Ilchester, Ilminster, and Crewkerne. To the north the limestone Mendip Hills are honeycombed with spectacular caves and gorges such as Wookey Hole and Cheddar Gorge. The magnificent cathedral city of Wells is within easy driving distance. *Directions:* From the M5 take exit 25 and continue 4 1/2 miles southeast to Hatch Beauchamp. Take the Station Road to Frog Street Farm.

FROG STREET FARM
Owner Veronica Cole
Beercrocombe
Taunton, Somerset TA3 6AF
Tel: (0823) 480430
3 rooms with private bathrooms
From £23 per person
Open March to October
Children over 12

The Old Schoolhouse is, as its name implies, a hotel and restaurant tastefully converted from an old school and a chapel. The dining room exudes simple country style with tables and chairs grouped around an open fire. Owner Ann Leighton terms her cuisine "imaginative," and typical dinner choices might include deep fried Brie in breadcrumbs, lamb cutlets with garlic sauce, and a selection of desserts. After dinner, guests can relax in the lounge with its inviting floral print sofas in front of a large fireplace. The bedrooms are unusually spacious: all have televisions, facilities for making tea and coffee, and ensuite bathrooms. Several of the very large rooms can accommodate up to two children on "put-you-up" beds. (Ann also has a cot for infants.) While a few of the rooms have sprigged wallpaper and matching coverlets and curtains, most are painted in soft pastels with matching flowered bedheads and curtains: very plain but most attractive. Two ground floor bedrooms can accommodate a wheelchair. The Old Schoolhouse is conveniently located adjacent to the gate leading to stately Berkeley Castle which is still lived in by the Berkeley family but is open for touring from spring to autumn. Next to the castle is the Jenner museum, devoted to the life and works of Edward Jenner who discovered the cure for smallpox. *Directions:* Exit the M5 at junction 14 and follow the A38 signposted to Gloucester for about 5 miles where you turn left to Berkeley.

THE OLD SCHOOLHOUSE
Owner Ann Leighton
Canonbury Street
Berkeley, Gloucestershire GL13 9BG
Tel: (0453) 811711
7 rooms with private bathrooms
From £37 single & £52 double
Closed 2 weeks after Christmas
Credit cards MC, VS
Children welcome

This well proportioned Victorian rectory is set in secluded grounds overlooking glorious vistas of the Derbyshire countryside. Geraldine and Stuart Worthington's solicitous welcome includes an invitation to the evening dinner party. Guests are introduced to each other over cocktails in the drawing room before sitting down to the large dining room table, beautifully laid with silver and crystal. Geraldine and Stuart dine with their guests; Geraldine serving unobtrusively with Stuart pouring the wine. After dinner, guests, host, and hostess return to the drawing room for port and coffee around the cheery log fire. The front bedroom has a large double bed framed by blue- and white-flowered draperies hung from a coronet, matching bedspread and bed ruffle, and an ensuite bathroom. The large twin room has thick bathrobes so guests can pop across the hall to their bathroom. The third twin room tucked under the eaves of the roof has a steeply sloping ceiling and adjacent luxurious shower room. The dramatic and rugged Derbyshire scenery is a strong attraction for walkers. Many visitors also tour Chatsworth House, Haddon Hall, and the open-air Monday market in Bakewell. *Directions:* Leave Ashbourne on the A523 towards Leek. In 2 miles turn right towards Ilam. Drive through Okeover Park and turn left as you go through the gates. In 2 miles, at Blore crossroads, turn left and The Old Rectory is on your right beyond the church.

THE OLD RECTORY
Owners Geraldine & Stuart Worthington
Blore
Ashbourne, Derbyshire DE6 2BS
Tel: (033529) 287
3 rooms with private bathrooms
From £29 per person
Closed Christmas
No children
Wolsey Lodge

This is primarily a Victorian rectory with spacious, high-ceilinged rooms with decorative plasterwork and tall windows. The dining room, however, dates back to the 16th century, and thus has a low-beamed ceiling and a large inglenook fireplace with a wood-burning stove. Here guests dine together by lamplight, feasting on Anthony's specialties such as a cheese and herb pate, cream of carrot and orange soup, coq au vin, and rhubarb pie. After dinner Anthony and Kathleen join their guests for coffee and conversation in the colorful drawing room. Breakfast is served on the sheltered terrace overlooking the garden lawn or, if the weather does not cooperate, guests are pampered with breakfast in bed. Bedrooms are large and comfortable, decorated with pretty wallpapers and matching drapes. Two have ensuite bathrooms while the third has the private use of the bathroom down the hall. Boltongate is on the quiet, northernmost fringes of the Lake District, an area offering many pretty villages such as Caldbeck, Borrowdale, Ullswater, Keswick, and Buttermere. William Wordsworth's birthplace is found nearby in Cockermouth. *Directions:* Leave the M6 at exit 40, bypass Keswick and take the A591 for 7 miles. At the Castle Inn turn right at the sign for Ireby. The Old Rectory is the first house in the village on your right.

THE OLD RECTORY
Owners Anthony & Kathleen Peacock
Boltongate, Cumbria CA5 1DA
Tel: (09657) 647
3 rooms with private bathrooms
From £29 per person
Closed Christmas & January
Credit cards all major
Children over 14
No Smoking house
Wolsey Lodge

From the outside, Hatpins looks like a well-kept suburban home, attractive but not especially different from other residences on the street. However, once inside, you will find this is a very special place because the owner, Mary Waller, a former designer of hats and wedding dresses, has combined her talent as a seamstress with a natural flair for decorating to transform her home into a delightfully inviting, "decorator-perfect" bed and breakfast. Now her talents are displayed in every room of the house in the drapes, pillows, and bed coverings which she has skillfully sewn from lovely fabrics. Her decor rivals that found in the most sophisticated manor house hotels. Enhancing the delightful decor is the warmth of Mary's hospitality; she loves to please her guests. Bosham is an especially appealing coastal town, and Old Bosham brims with charm: it is great fun to wander down to the waterfront and explore the tiny lanes--be sure not to miss the old church which is depicted in the Bayeux Tapestry. Also nearby are Portsmouth, where you can visit the *HMS Victory* and the *Mary Rose*, and the cathedral city of Chichester with its lovely harbor. A few miles inland is Goodwood House, and The Weald and Downland Museum, a collection of very old cottages and buildings. *Directions:* From Chichester take the A259 west for 3 miles to Bosham. Hatpins is on the main road into town.

HATPINS
Owner Mary Waller
Bosham Lane, Old Bosham
Chichester, Sussex PO18 8HG
Tel: (0243) 572644
4 rooms with private bathrooms
From £20 per person
Open all year
Children welcome
No Smoking house

Visitors come to Pethills Bank Cottage to visit the sights in the region, and return because this bed and breakfast is the most delightful place to stay. Set high on a hill surrounded by fields, the cottage sits snug in an acre of rolling gardens overlooking the countryside. The cozy living room has thick, golden stone walls and a large picture window framing the rolling lawn and rockery garden. The bedrooms are unexpectedly large, decorated in an unobtrusive modern style that gives them a light, airy, and uncluttered feel. Each has an ensuite bathroom and a host of "extras": biscuit jar brimming with tempting goodies, fruit bowl, mineral water, iron, hairdryer, remote control TV, shampoo, and bath oil. The Garden Room opens up to a veranda which overlooks the fields, The Dales Room also has magnificent countryside views and the largest bathroom. The Cottage Room has old-world charm with a beamed ceiling and low windows. Breakfast fortifies you for the entire day as it includes an array of fruits, crisp bacon, sausage, eggs, tomatoes, and mushrooms, and toast with homemade jam and marmalade. Yvonne helps guests plan visits to the Potteries factories and "seconds" shops (for example Coalport, Royal Doulton, Minton, Spode, and Wedgwood). Derbyshire's dales and historic houses Chatsworth and Haddon are close at hand. *Directions:* Bottomhouse is on the A523 between Leek and Ashbourne. Turn into the lane opposite the Little Chef restaurant and follow the signs up the hill for about a mile.

PETHILLS BANK COTTAGE
Owners Yvonne & Richard Martin
Bottomhouse
Leek, Staffordshire ST13 7PF
Tel: (0538) 304235/304555 fax: (0538) 304575
3 rooms with private bathrooms
From £17 per person
Closed Christmas
Children welcome

This exquisite home takes its name from the Bourne Eau stream that runs alongside its grounds, separating it from an ancient abbey and a park. This house has evolved over the years and Dawn and George Bishop have decorated each room according to its historical period. The Elizabethan dining room has a flagstone floor topped with an oriental carpet and a trestle table set before a huge inglenook fireplace beneath a low-beamed ceiling. The high-ceilinged, formal Georgian drawing room has enviable antiques and the snug Jacobean music room has a concert piano and a cheery log fire blazing in the ornately carved fireplace. Guests enjoy a scrumptious cooked breakfast in the low-ceilinged breakfast room furnished in mellow country pine. Bedrooms are equally lovely; the enormous Master Suite has a large sitting area around a fireplace whose mantle was once part of the abbey's altar and an adjacent dressing room with a single bed; the smaller Jacobean Room with its period bed has a glorious modern bathroom; and the large twin-bedded Georgian Room has a private staircase and views across the vast lawns. The landscape around the nearby town of Spalding is ablaze with red and yellow tulips in the spring, and gently rolling wolds lead north to Lincoln with its cobbled streets, majestic hilltop cathedral, and castle. *Directions:* Bourne is on the A15 between Peterborough and Sleaford. The concealed entrance is on the A15, 200 yards south of the main traffic lights in the middle of town, opposite the park.

BOURNE EAU HOUSE
Owners Dawn & George Bishop
Bourne, Lincolnshire PE10 9LY
Tel: (0778) 423621
3 rooms with private bathrooms
From £25 per person
Closed Christmas
Children welcome
Wolsey Lodge

Willmead Farm is a wonderfully endearing thatched cottage nestled in a sheltered glen; a perfectly idyllic setting. Willmead has three simply decorated bedrooms grouped around a minstrels' gallery that overlooks the entrance hall. The twin-bedded room has an ensuite bathroom while the two doubles share the facilities of two bathrooms. Low-beamed ceilings and old-fashioned board doors with metal latches add to the appeal of this storybook house. Comfortable sofas and chairs are grouped around the fireplace in the sitting room and beyond is the dining room where guests gather in the morning around the large table. A scrumptious farmhouse breakfast that includes homemade jams is the only meal that Hilary serves. However, Hilary has compiled a book of local restaurants' menus so guests can choose where to dine. For a sinfully rich Devon cream tea, detour round the duck pond and follow the path that leads past the barn to the thatched hamlet of Lustleigh. The wild beauty of Dartmoor with its sheltered villages and market towns, wild ponies, and spectacular scenery is a magnet for walkers and those touring by car. *Directions:* From Exeter take the A38 towards Plymouth and exit at the A382 but do not go into Bovey Tracey: stay on the A382 Lustleigh road. After 2 miles you pass a phone box on your right and take the first narrow lane on the left for half a mile to Willmead.

WILLMEAD FARM
Owner Hilary Roberts
Bovey Tracey
Newton Abbot, Devon TQ13 9NP
Tel: (06477) 214
3 rooms, 1 with private bathroom
From £19 per person
Closed Christmas
Children over 12
No Smoking house

Bradford Old Windmill ceased to function as a mill many years ago; the sails have gone but the stone tower remains, albeit modernized and extended in recent years to provide more extensive accommodation. Priscilla and Peter were unfortunately on holiday at the time of my visit to the Old Windmill, but their personalities seemed to shine through in the decor of their home. Rooms are furnished with an eclectic mixture of modern, antique, and folksy furniture and decorated with a fascinating clutter of everything from old bones to railway memorabilia, filling every nook and cranny. Guests gather for breakfast around a large old pine table. Priscilla is also happy to provide an evening vegetarian meal if guests so desire. Up the narrow staircase the four bedrooms vary greatly in size and decor. Masses of dark wooden beams criss-cross to the high peaked ceiling of the Oval Room where a pine bed topped with a bright patchwork quilt sits center stage. The Family Room has thick stone walls and deeply set windows overlooking the town and offers an unusual oval bed plus a small sofa that can be converted to additional sleeping accommodation. *Directions:* Take the A363 from Bath to Bradford on Avon. As the road drops steeply into the town turn left up the first small driveway. Parking is "tight" but Priscilla and Peter are happy to assist guests who are not used to maneuvering their cars.

BRADFORD OLD WINDMILL
Owners Peter & Priscilla Roberts
4 Masons Lane
Bradford on Avon, Wiltshire BA15 1QN
Tel: (02216) 6842
4 rooms with private bathrooms
From £16 to £25 per person
Open all year
Children over 12
No Smoking house

Priory Steps, a row of 17th-century weavers' cottages high above the town of Bradford on Avon, is a glorious place to stay. The village tumbles down the hill to the banks of the River Avon, its narrow streets full of interesting shops and antique dealers. A few miles distant, the glories of Bath await exploration and are easily accessible by car or the local train service. Hostess Diana is a gourmet cook and guests dine "en famille" in the traditionally furnished dining room. While Diana's cooking is reason enough to spend several days here, the adjacent library with its books and pamphlets highlighting the many places to visit in the area provides additional justification. The bedrooms are all very different, each accented with antique furniture, and all have smart modern bathrooms, TV, and tea and coffee tray. The Blue Room has large shuttered and curtained windows and a pleasing decor in shades of blue, while the large English Room has striped paper in muted tones of green coordinating with flowered curtains. There is a touch of whimsy in the bathroom of the dark-beamed Frog Room where the odd frog or two has inspired former guests to send their own contributions to an ever-growing collection of the creatures. The frogless bedroom itself it very pretty. *Directions*: Take the A363 from Bath to Bradford on Avon. As the road drops steeply into the town, Newtown is the first road to the right. Priory Steps is 150 yards on the left.

PRIORY STEPS
Owners Carey & Diana Chapman
Newtown
Bradford on Avon, Wiltshire BA15 1NQ
Tel: (02216) 2230
5 rooms with private bathrooms
From £38 single & £52 double
Open all year
Children over 12
Wolsey Lodge

It is easily understandable why the tiny hamlet of Avoncliff, on the banks of the Avon river, surrounded by wooded hills, is a magnet on summer weekends and evenings. Isolated from the hubbub by large wrought iron gates, Weavers Mill was originally built as a grist mill, then converted to a fulling mill for the wool trade in 1763. The adjacent river Avon rushes over the weir which once provided power for the mill's turbine, but inside the roar is muted to dulcet tones by the thick brick walls. A large double room has an ensuite bathroom while the two smaller double rooms share the other two upstairs bathrooms or use the small shower room downstairs. All the bedrooms have tea and coffee trays and are decorated with homey simplicity. Breakfast is served at the dining room table which looks across the weir; guests usually go for dinner to the adjacent Cross Guns pub. It is a very pleasant evening stroll along the tow path into Bradford on Avon. Across the bridge spanning the Avon the local train station operates a frequent service into nearby Bath. *Directions:* Head south from Bradford on Avon towards Frome for half a mile, then as soon as you cross the canal turn sharp right and follow the narrow country lane upwards till you come to a sharp right turn beside a cottage signposted Arncliff. Go down the steep hill to the very bottom, turn sharp right under the aqueduct, pass the Cross Guns pub and the road dead-ends at the mill.

WEAVERS MILL
Owner Margaret Simpson
Avoncliff
Bradford on Avon, Wiltshire BA15 2HB
Tel: (02216) 5128
4 rooms with private bathrooms
From £18 per person
Open April to November
Children over 12
No Smoking house

Deep in the Devon countryside, in a 16th-century stone and cob farmhouse called Lower Beers, Anne Nicholls has realized her dream and founded "Bonne Bouche," a residential cooking school. Here she and her husband Gerald provide guests an idyllic spot to perfect their culinary skills. Course offerings range from weekends designed to remove the angst from entertaining to an in-depth four-week course. Her approach is both creative and practical, a handy combination. The Nicholls also welcome guests who are simply on holiday; spending their days exploring the lush Devon countryside and enjoying delicious candlelit dinners in the evenings. The comfortable sitting room offers guests an inviting sofa and chairs in front of the enormous fireplace as well as an assortment of books and magazines. Bedrooms are named after herbs and are fresh and clean, with flower-sprigged bedcovers and matching draperies or wallpapers. Some sightseeing options are to explore Dartmoor and Exmoor and to visit the National Trust properties of Knight Hayes and Killerton. *Directions:* Lower Beers is only five minutes from the motorway. Leave the M5 at exit 28 and turn into Cullompton. At the first T-junction turn right towards Willand on the B3181. In 1 mile, just before the pylons, turn left to Brithem Bottom. Lower Beers is the second house on the left after 1 mile.

LOWER BEERS
Owners Anne & Gerald Nicholls
Brithem Bottom
Cullompton, Devon EX15 1NB
Tel: (0884) 32257
6 rooms with private bathrooms
From £25 per person
Closed Christmas
Children over 14
No Smoking house
Wolsey Lodge

Gently rolling hills where sheep graze peacefully and shaded valleys with meandering streams surround the picturesque villages of Chipping Campden and Broad Campden where The Malt House hugs the quiet main street. Years ago barley was made into malt here for brewing beer. Now it is a picturesque guesthouse that provides a perfect central location for exploring other Cotswold villages. A quiet sitting room invites browsing through books and magazines. If requested in advance, a four-course dinner is served on a long table before a massive inglenook fireplace and mullioned windows which offer glimpses of sheep at pasture in the orchard. All the bedrooms except a small single room face the garden, so guests are ensured a quiet night's repose. The rooms all have plenty of country-cottage charm, and those which have bathrooms across the hall are considerably less expensive than those where facilities are ensuite. One bedroom has a lovely four-poster, another a grand brass bed, and all have televisions and tea and coffee trays. Lovely Cotswold villages to explore include Chipping Campden, Bourton-on-the-Water, Upper and Lower Slaughter, Stow-on-the-Wold, Bibury, and Broadway. Garden lovers will enjoy Kiftsgate, Hidcote Manor, and Batsford. *Directions:* On entering Chipping Campden take the first right; you know you are in Broad Campden when you see The Bakers Arms. The Malt House is opposite the wall topped by a tall topiary hedge.

THE MALT HOUSE
Owner Pat Robinson
Broad Campden
Chipping Campden, Gloucestershire GL55 6UU
Tel: (0386) 840295
5 rooms, 4 with private bathrooms
From £55 double
Closed Christmas
Children welcome

Centrally located in the middle of this picturesque Cotswold town but on a quiet side street, Cowley House offers bed and breakfast accommodation in a tastefully converted grain barn and the adjoining farmer's cottage. Mary takes great pride in her establishment where her rooms are all freshly papered and painted and have an airy and unpretentious style. Uneven flagstone floors, stripped pine doors, and the occasional old wooden beam running though the wall or supporting the ceiling add to the country ambience. Three of the bedrooms have private bathrooms. A large family bedroom in the former grain barn has an ensuite toilet and sink and uses the shower in an upstairs bathroom. Several of the rooms have televisions and Mary is happy to bring tea or coffee to guests in the comfortable sitting room which overlooks the front garden. Mary's husband Robert has a jewelry shop in the High Street and he also specializes in antique clock restoration. Surrounding Broadway are the lovely Cotswold villages and towns with appealing names such as Chipping Campden, Upper and Lower Slaughter, Stow-on-the-Wold, Bourton-on-the-Water, and Upper and Lower Swell. Stratford-upon-Avon, Worcester, Bath, and Oxford are all within an hour's driving distance. *Directions:* Broadway is on the A44 between Evesham and Stow-on-the-Wold. From Broadway High Street take the Snowshill road and Cowley House is the first house on your right.

COWLEY HOUSE
Owners Mary & Robert Kemp
Church Street
Broadway, Worcestershire WR12 7AE
Tel: (0386) 853262
6 rooms, 3 with private bathrooms
From single £15, double £33 to £45
Closed Christmas
Children welcome
No Smoking house

Luigi Bellorini came to England many years ago to learn the language. It took him longer than he thought and, while struggling to conjugate his verbs, he fell in love with an English girl, married, and made Britain his home. The desire to cook his national food in his own restaurant lingered and after his children were grown Luigi and his wife Pauline took the plunge and moved to Broadway at the heart of the Cotswolds. Now every evening Luigi can be found in his kitchen creating dinner, yet still finding time to come to tables and have a special little chat with each of his patrons. Italian food lovers will be delighted by both the set and a la carte menus, though it must be emphasized that the menu is not limited to Italian food nor the wine list to Italian wine. After a satisfying meal and a nightcap in the residents' bar, guests can retire up the narrow staircase or across the courtyard to their room. Bedrooms are not fancy but they are prettily decorated and there is an extra room up a steep flight of stairs for children. Broadway is one of the Cotswolds' most crowded villages but Luigi's guests need not worry about parking as there is a private car park at the bottom of the garden. A stay at Milestone House allows visitors to experience the picturesque town of Broadway in the less crowded hours of early morning and evening. *Directions:* Broadway is on the A44 between Evesham and Stow-on-the-Wold.

MILESTONE HOUSE
Owners Luigi & Pauline Bellorini
122 High Street
Broadway, Worcestershire WR12 7AJ
Tel: (0386) 853432
4 rooms with private bathrooms
From £24 per person (no singles)
Closed Christmas
Credit cards MC, VS
Children welcome

The picturesque beauty of the village of Broadway is world famous, and as it is located in the heart of the Cotswolds, it is often crowded with visitors. Just a half mile from the hubbub lies Mill Hay House, a lovely old home with some parts dating back to 1705 set in over an acre of manicured grounds where birdsong is the only noise which interrupts the utter tranquility of the setting. The owner, Hans Will, lives primarily in Germany while his friendly managers Netta and Ben Gibson offer guests a warm welcome to Mill Hay House. The four large double rooms look out through stone mullioned windows across the garden, all beautifully furnished with fine period furniture. A grand four-poster bed and a balcony overlooking the adjacent millpond is a feature of one room. Another room has a lovely old wooden bed set before a large stone fireplace with an electric fire; just right for toasting cold toes on a chilly winter evening. Single travelers enjoy the 18th-century single four-poster bed in the small bedroom. The gardens are a treat and lead down to the old mill with its creeper-covered waterwheel. On a clear day you can see for miles from the top of the nearby 18th-century Broadway Tower and inside there is a museum with interesting displays including one on William Morris the designer. *Directions:* Broadway is on the A44 between Evesham and Stow-on-the-Wold. From Broadway High Street take the Snowshill road and Mill Hay House is half a mile down on the right.

MILL HAY HOUSE
Managers Netta & Ben Gibson
Snowshill Road
Broadway, Worcestershire WR12 7JS
Tel: (0386) 852498
5 rooms sharing 2 bathrooms
From £30 single, £50 to £60 double
Closed January & February
Children welcome

This 15th-century cottage lies in the tiny hamlet of Westbrook, one blink and you're through it, on the outskirts of Bromham. Gloria and Richard Steed live in the main cottage where guests have their own entrance to the country-style breakfast room and adjoining information nook packed with information booklets and tourist pamphlets. Guest accommodation is in three rustic-style bedrooms in the adjoining converted wood-sided barn. The two double and one twin-bedded rooms have lots of beams, small shower bathrooms, televisions, and tea and coffee trays. The Steeds are keen gardeners and on their 2 acres they have a walled garden, a wild garden, a fun putting green (which guests are encouraged to use), an arbor kitchen garden, and a herbaceous border that contains rare and old-fashioned species of plants. There are many interesting sights close by such as the picturesque villages of Lacock and Castle Combe, Devizes with its open stall and cattle market (Thursdays), Avebury (the largest stone circle in Europe), Stonehenge, Salisbury, and Bath. The Cottage is an unsophisticated bed and breakfast for travellers seeking simpler accommodation at an affordable price. *Directions:* From London exit the M4 at junction 16 and take the A3102 through Calne towards Melksham. The cottage is signposted on your right in the hamlet of Westbrook.

THE COTTAGE
Owners Richard & Gloria Steed
Westbrook, Bromham
Chippenham, Wiltshire SN15 2EE
Tel: (0380) 850255
3 rooms with private bathrooms
From £19 per person
Open March to November
Children welcome

The Buck Inn is a traditional old Georgian coaching inn full of old-world charm. It stands beneath the towering craggy heights of Buckden Pike which rises steeply to 2,300 feet behind the inn. Conviviality and good cheer are the order of the day in the bar where real ale is hand-pulled from the cool stone cellars. In summer there is always a crowd and overnight guests may prefer the quieter restaurant in a bright enclosed courtyard where in days of old sheep auctions were held. You can enjoy a set four-course dinner with lots of choices for each course or order from the extensive bar menu salads, sandwiches, grills, fish, homemade pies, and traditional English fare. Bedrooms are country-style in their decor, the largest being a four-poster room with a high, raftered ceiling. The surrounding rugged countryside offers many paths for walkers: long day hikes as well as shorter strolls. Wharfedale has several lovely, mellow, stone villages such as Grassington, Appletreewick, and Kettlewell. It is a spectacular drive from here through Coverdale to Middleham with its ruined castle and on to Jervaulx with its romantic ruined abbey. To the west, moorland roads lead to Arncliffe and Littondale and on to Malham (in Airedale) famous for its massive crags, tarn, and cove. *Directions:* Buckden is 18 miles north of Skipton on the B6160.

THE BUCK INN
Owners Phoebe & Trevor Illingworth
Buckden
Skipton, Yorkshire, BD23 5JA
Tel: (075676) 227 fax: (075676) 241
15 rooms with private bathrooms
From £26 per person
Open all year
Credit cards MC, VS
Children welcome

Built over a century ago, Chilvester Hill House is a solidly constructed Victorian home isolated from the busy A4 by a large garden. John and Gill Dilley retired here and subsequently unretired themselves; John, a physician, now works as an occupational health consultant and Gill entertains guests and breeds beef cattle. Gill enjoys cooking and a typical (optional) dinner might consist of smoked trout, lamb noisettes with vegetables from the garden, fruit fool, and cheese and biscuits. They have a short wine list with over 20 French and German wines. A soft pastel decor, treasured antiques, and a cleverly displayed collection of commemorative plates make the large, high-ceilinged drawing room the most elegant room in the house. The bedrooms are spacious, high-ceilinged rooms, each individually decorated with flowery Sanderson wallpaper. All have mineral water, tea and coffee tray, TV, tourist information, and private bathroom. Visitors can enjoy the heated swimming pool during the summer months or take advantage of John and Gill's mimeographed maps marked with scenic routes to nearby Castle Combe, Lacock, and the Avebury Neolithic Circle. Bath, Oxford, and Salisbury are an easy drive away. *Directions:* From London leave the M4 at junction 16 and take the A3102 to Calne. Turn right on the A4 west towards Chippenham. After half a mile turn right (signposted Bremhill) and immediately right into the drive.

CHILVESTER HILL HOUSE
Owners John & Gill Dilley
Calne, Wiltshire SN11 0LP
Tel: (0249) 813981 Fax: (0249) 814217
3 rooms with private bathrooms
From £30 per person
Open all year
Credit cards all major
Children over 12
Wolsey Lodge

Because of its quiet country location just 3 miles off the motorway, almost equidistant between Edinburgh and London, New Capernwray Farm is an ideal place to break a long, tiring journey. However, many weary travellers return for a proper country getaway to explore this unspoiled area. There really is nothing "new" about this solid, whitewashed stone farmhouse, for, despite its name, it is approaching its 300th birthday. It was bought in 1974 by Sally and Peter Townsend who supervised its complete refurbishment while preserving its lovely old features and now offer a very warm welcome to their guests. Before dinner guests enjoy sherry in the cozy sitting room in front of a cheerful fire and then proceed to the dining room for a candlelit dinner. Bedrooms are particularly light, bright, and cheerful in their decor. The largest bedroom spans the breadth of the house, has a bathroom tucked neatly under the eaves and, as in all the rooms, is well equipped with tea, coffee, biscuits, hairdryer, mints, and a substantial sewing kit. The twin-bedded rooms have bathrooms down the hall. Sally has a wealth of well-used books and maps about the area's walks, the Lake District, and the Yorkshire Dales. *Directions:* Leave the M6 at junction 35 and from the roundabout follow signs for Over Kellet/Kirkby Lonsdale. Turn left at the T-junction for the short drive into Over Kellet. Turn left at the village green: after 2 miles the farm is on the left

NEW CAPERNWRAY FARM
Owners Sally & Peter Townsend
Capernwray
Carnforth, Lancashire LA6 1AD
Tel: (0524) 734284
3 rooms with private bathrooms
From £24.50 per person
Closed Christmas
Children over 10
Wolsey Lodge

Fronting the main street of Castle Hedingham, The Old Schoolhouse is now a charming little cottage. Its front door opens directly into the dining room where a well-polished table sits on a cool flagstone floor beneath a low-beamed ceiling and inviting chairs are drawn up around an inglenook fireplace. A narrow arch leads to the sitting room, its French windows opening to the most flower-filled garden in this guide. When Penny came here several years ago the garden was a rough field but now is a luxuriant mass of plants and trees terracing up past an ornamental pond filled with carp, exotic fish, and tiny toads whose night-time serenades fill the air. Scented creepers climb towards the upper-story windows of the little cottage in the garden where two narrow bedrooms are tucked under the steeply sloping eaves. The larger bedroom has a small sitting area, twin beds, and a sunny ensuite bathroom, while the other bedroom has its bathroom downstairs. The bedroom in the main house overlooks the village tennis courts. With several days' notice Penny is happy to cook dinner. There are two very nice pubs and a restaurant in the village. During the summer you can tour the village castle and Penny encourages a stroll down to the picturesque parish church. Cambridge is a 40-minute drive, while Constable country lies closer at hand. *Directions:* From Colchester take the A604 to Sible Hedingham and the B1058 to Castle Hedingham.

THE OLD SCHOOLHOUSE
Owner Penny Crawshaw
St James Street
Castle Hedingham, Essex CO9 3EW
Tel: (0787) 61370
3 rooms with private bathrooms
From £22.50 per person
Closed Christmas
Children over 12
No Smoking house

Just up the hill from the delightful Dartmoor town of Chagford is the former rectory that is now Bly House, a very old-fashioned, English, family-run bed and breakfast. I was pleased by the excellent value for money that it offers. The house is absolutely packed with Victorian furnishings and Mrs. Thompson's extensive collections of Victorian china and delicate glassware are displayed throughout the house. Owing to these fragile and valuable decorations, small children are understandably not encouraged as guests. The lounge, with its view of the garden, provides a comfortable retreat and lots of collectibles to admire. The spacious bedrooms are a perfect backdrop for Victorian furniture and some of the bedrooms have elegant four-posters and half-tester beds. For dinner there are several old-world pubs in Chagford, and, for walking or sightseeing, the wildly beautiful Dartmoor countryside is close at hand. Ponies and sheep graze in the fields, the hills are topped by wind-sculpted granite outcroppings, and delightful little villages such as Widecombe in the Moor and North Bovey nestle in wooded valleys. *Directions:* From Exeter take the A30 to Whiddon Down, then turn left on the A382 for the 5-mile drive to Chagford. Turn left in Chagford Square, passing the Three Crowns on your right. Turn left at the Globe Hotel and Bly House is the second house on the right.

BLY HOUSE
Owners Geoffrey & Esme Thompson
Nattadon Hill
Chagford, Devon TQ13 8BW
Tel: (06473) 2404
7 rooms with private bathrooms
From £20 per person
Closed November to mid-January
Children over 12

Thruxted Oast, conveniently located about a 10-minute drive south of Canterbury, like so many fine old buildings, was in a most dilapidated condition before being rescued by Hilary and Tim Derouet and transformed into a lovely home. The ground floor has a dining room and a rather formal parlor, but the heart of the house is the family-style kitchen where guests gather each morning at a large antique farmhouse table for a delicious breakfast. Upstairs the three guest bedrooms are cleverly converted from the three original drying stalls with their high peaked wooden ceilings and massive rafters. These spacious twin-bedded rooms are attractively papered with a tiny print design which is complemented by pretty short drapes at the windows. The same pattern is repeated in the handmade patchwork quilts, throw pillows, and dressing table skirts; my favorite room, Chaucer, features soft pink and green tones. Tim used to be a farmer and his green thumb can be seen in the lovely garden stretching behind the oast where abundant flowers border a lovely green lawn. *Directions:* From Canterbury take the A28 towards Ashford. On the city outskirts cross the A2 and after 200 yards turn left on St Nicholas Road. At the end T-junction, turn right. Continue 2 miles, past St Augustine Hospital. Continue straight over the cross road and down the hill to Thruxted Oast on the right.

THRUXTED OAST
Owners Hilary & Tim Derouet
Chartham
Canterbury, Kent CT4 7BX
Tel: (0227) 730080
3 rooms with private bathrooms
From £65 double
Closed Christmas
Credit cards all major
Children over 12

This storybook farmhouse surrounded by miles and miles of rolling Devon countryside and reached by a typical narrow lane lined by tall hedges has that end-of-the-earth feel to it; yet in actuality it is only 9 miles from the busy city of Exeter. Higher Perry Farm is no longer a working farm but the Watsons still keep an assortment of ducks, geese, hens, sheep, and horses and two friendly dogs who love to romp through the fields. The large, low-ceilinged, beamed country kitchen is the heart of the house where meals are served "en famille" at the long pine table as Jane and Tony enjoy getting to know their guests by eating dinner with them. A typical dinner might be smoked trout, roast lamb with all the trimmings, dessert, and cheese. Afterwards guests relax in the sitting room and enjoy coffee. The two bedrooms, a double and a twin, are located downstairs off the sitting room, and they share the facilities of the bathroom that lies between them. During the day, guests enjoy the heated swimming pool in the Watsons' garden or pleasurable walking and driving in this region midway between Dartmoor and Exmoor. *Directions:* Leave the M5 at junction 27, take the A373 to Tiverton and the A3072 towards Crediton. After passing the UK petrol station, turn right onto a narrow country lane to Cheriton Fitzpane. Turn left at the village church (the road is signposted Crediton) and after 1 mile turn left at the top of a steep hill, cross the cattle grid, and follow the drive to Higher Perry Farm.

HIGHER PERRY FARM
Owners Jane & Tony Watson
Cheriton Fitzpane
Crediton, Devon EX17 4BO
Tel: (03636) 573
2 rooms sharing 1 bathroom
From £18 per person
Closed Christmas
Children welcome

The Tudor Farmhouse is a picturesque, small, comfortable hotel in the pretty village of Clearwell, located just on the edge of the vast Forest of Dean. Oliver Cromwell is said to have stayed here during a hunting trip. There are two inviting public rooms, the richly paneled sitting room with flowered sofas and comfy chairs grouped before the large fireplace and the sunny conservatory overlooking the courtyard. The dining room is country-elegant with rose-colored tablecloths, warm stone walls, and flickering candlelight. The a la carte menu offers dishes made from fresh, local ingredients. The three bedrooms in the main house are at the top of the dark, polished, spiral staircase behind low, latched doors. These cozy rooms have tiny mullioned windows and are furnished in traditional style, mainly with reproduction antiques. Three more bedrooms are found in an old cider press in the courtyard: a large, charming attic room above and two smaller, plainer rooms below. Guests come here to enjoy the peace and quiet of the countryside and the forest which is in full glory in the autumn. Clearwell also has Roman iron mines and caves to visit and an interesting "Puzzle Wood" where trees sprout from huge boulders. Nearby are the attractive market town of Ross-on-Wye and the spectacular gorge at Symonds Yat. *Directions:* Take the M4 from Bristol over the Severn Bridge to exit 22 signed Monmouth. Follow the A466 for 7 miles, then turn right over the Bigsweir bridge for Clearwell.

TUDOR FARMHOUSE HOTEL
Owners Sheila & James Reid
Clearwell
Coleford, Gloucestershire GL16 8JS
Tel: (0594) 33046
9 rooms with private bathrooms
From £21 per person
Open all year
Children welcome (not in the restaurant)

This pretty village of flint-walled, tile-roofed cottages is no longer "next-the-sea," but separated from it by a vast saltwater marsh formed as the sea retreated. The massive structure of Cley Mill stands as a handsome monument to man's ability to harness the forces of nature. Guests enter the Mill directly into the beamed dining room decorated with country-style pine furniture. The circular sitting room has large chintz chairs drawn round a stone fireplace whose mantle is a sturdy beam displaying toby jugs. Stacked above the sitting room are two large circular bedrooms with ensuite bathrooms; the Wheat Chamber is where the grain was stored and the Stone Room is where the massive grinding stones crushed the flour. Two additional small bedrooms share a bathroom. During the day the mill is open to the public to visit the observation room and the wooden cap of the mill with its massive gears and complex mechanisms that once turned the grinding stones. The old boathouse and stables in the yard have been converted into small, self-catering cottages. Birdwatching, sailing, cycling, and walking are popular pastimes in the area. The seaside towns of Sheringham, Cromer, and Wells are close at hand. There are a great many stately homes to explore such as Sandringham House, the Royal Family's country residence, Jacobean Fellbrigg Hall, Holkham, and Blickling Hall. *Directions:* From King's Lynn follow the A149 around the coast to Cley-next-the-Sea, where the windmill is well signposted.

CLEY MILL GUEST HOUSE
Manager Carolyn Hederman
Cley-next-the-Sea
Holt, Norfolk NR25 7NN
Tel: (0263) 740209
4 rooms, 2 with private bathrooms
From £25 per person
Open March to mid-January
Children over 6

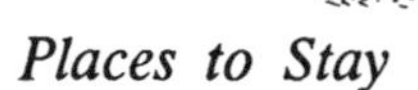

Gorgeous pastoral scenery aside, there can be no better reason to visit an area than outstanding food, which is what Richard and Anne Arbuthnot provide at Clun Old Post Office. Meals here are a delight--this little restaurant has earned the prestigious Michelin red M. Diners make their selections while sitting before the fire in what was once the postmistress's parlor. They may then dine in either the shop-front, with a view of village life passing by, or in the conservatory, where large glass windows offer a view across the village rooftops to the countryside. Dining is a la carte with every dish freshly cooked to order: some six starters (filo asparagus tart and layered lambs sweetbreads, for example), even more main courses (from fillet of beef to aubergine and artichoke puff), and even more puddings (the indecisive can opt for a platter selection of everything). The long wine list includes Australian and New Zealand wines as well as European. Two simply decorated bedrooms sharing the facilities of a large bathroom are let only to those who come to dine. In between breakfast and dinner you'll find lots of things to do in the area to whet your appetite: walking the hills, exploring Ludlow and Shrewsbury, and visiting the Ironbridge Gorge museums. *Directions:* Take the A49 from Ludlow for 7 miles to Craven Arms, turn left on the B4368 for the 9-mile drive to Clun. The Old Post Office is in the center of the village on the left.

CLUN OLD POST OFFICE RESTAURANT
Owners Richard & Anne Arbuthnot
9 The Square
Clun, Shropshire SY7 8JA
Tel: (05884) 687
2 rooms sharing 1 bathroom
From £19 per person
Closed Monday, Tuesday, Christmas & February
Credit cards MC, VS
No children

Littlewell Farm hugs the roadside 1 mile south of the city of Wells. During the day, traffic rushes by as tourists and locals scamper between Glastonbury and Wells, but in the evening the hubbub ceases and the farm stands tranquil among fields on the outskirts of the village of Coxley. Host Gerry who hails from Germany and his Spanish wife Di have converted this 200-year-old farm into a cozy bed and breakfast. Duke, a large golden retriever, heralds guest arrivals, followed by the appearance of Gerry or Di and the offer of a welcoming pot of tea. This refreshment, or, if desired, a scrumptious cream tea, is enjoyed in the cottage-style sitting room with its old-fashioned flower-print chairs grouped around the coffee table. Watch your head as you climb the narrow staircase to the bedrooms, each tucked neatly under the eaves. For those who have difficulty with stairs, request the small downstairs double room. All of the bedrooms have a television and tea and coffee tray. The majority of the shower/bathrooms are very compact and this is to be expected, as Littlewell Farm is not a home of large proportions. Gerry is an enthusiastic cook and, apart from copious breakfasts, is, with advance notice, happy to prepare a most enjoyable three-course dinner. Nearby Wells is a tourist "must," its magnificent cathedral famous for its 14th-century clock where figures strike the hours and its moated Bishop's Palace where swans once rang a bell to be fed. *Directions:* Littlewell Farm is on the A39 1 mile south of Wells.

LITTLEWELL FARM
Owners Gerry & Di Gnoyke
Coxley
Wells, Somerset BA5 1QP
Tel: (0749) 77914
5 rooms with private bathrooms
From £16.50 per person
Open all year
Children over 12

We covered quite a few miles exploring the quaint villages of North Yorkshire in search of an inn that would reflect the atmosphere of the region. We happily ended our search in Coxwold, one of the prettiest villages in the area, its stone cottages separated from the village street by broad grass verges. In the midst of the village lies the Fauconberg Arms, a 17th-century stone inn packed with old-world charm, oak beams, a warm character, and a friendly atmosphere. It has a popular pub and good restaurant which is frequented by a very jovial crowd. Dick and Tricia Goodall are your hosts and they have carefully decorated four snug bedrooms, two doubles and two twins, with dainty prints in matching wallpapers and fabrics. One bedroom has a private shower and the rest share facilities. The surrounding village and region offer many options for sightseeing, including Shandy Hall, former home of Coxwold's eccentric parson, author Lawrence Stern. Travelling northwest to the next village, Kilburn, one may watch hand carvers make beautiful oak furniture, each piece incorporating a small carved mouse as a symbol of quiet industry. At the gateway to the North Yorkshire moors and adjacent to the magnificent ruins of Rievaulx Abbey is the gray stone, red-roofed market town of Helmsley with its smart shops and boutiques. A short drive to the east leads to Castle Howard where "Brideshead Revisited" was filmed. *Directions:* From York take the A19 towards Thirsk. Coxwold is between Easingwold and Thirsk.

FAUCONBERG ARMS
Owners Tricia & Richard Goodall
Coxwold
Yorkshire Y06 4AD
Tel: (03476) 214
4 rooms, 1 with ensuite shower
From £22.50 per person
Open all year
Children welcome

Host Michael Nightingale is an actor and his easy, welcoming manner and warm personality make you feel a valued guest at his home, The Thatched Cottage. This adorable 16th-century cobb cottage boasts tranquil views across rolling farmland to Haytor and distant Dartmoor. With its blackened beams and low ceilings, the sitting room offers a country-cozy welcome. The most appealing bedroom is located in this very old part of the cottage. The remaining two bedrooms are incorporated into a 20th-century extension where there is an airy twin room and, up a steep, open-tread stairway, another large bedroom which, though plain, is great for families. One of the nice features of The Thatched Cottage is that children are made very welcome and the Nightingales have a crib, high-chair, and extra folding bed on hand. By special arrangement, Daphne cooks dinners which may include fish, steak, roast lamb, or beef as a main course--guests are encouraged to bring their own wine. Breakfast is ordered the night before and Daphne has it waiting for you at your chosen time. A book in every bedroom offers an extensive list of recommended restaurants, pubs, museums, stately homes, and places of interest. The Thatched Cottage is a good location for exploring the two coasts and the wild moorlands of Dartmoor. *Directions:* Leave Crediton on the A3770. After 1 mile turn left towards Colford, and left into the Thatched Cottage's driveway.

THE THATCHED COTTAGE
Owners Michael & Daphne Nightingale
Barnstaple Cross
Crediton, Devon EX17 2EW
Tel: (03632) 3115
3 rooms with private bathrooms
From £18.50 per person
Closed December
Children welcome
No Smoking house

Hosts Michael and Eileen Wilkes offer their guests a warm and genuine welcome to their old farmhouse which dates from 1580. One is transported back in time upon entering this farmhouse where uneven, sloping plank floors, low beams, and an inglenook fireplace evoke a long-ago time. This is an idyllic country retreat where one could happily spend a long summer's evening reading in the garden, exploring the Norman church across the road, or doing nothing more energetic than competing in a game of clockwork golf on the lawn. Eileen has quite a reputation for her cooking; one of her most requested main courses is a traditional roast leg of lamb with fresh vegetables: however, arrangements must be made in advance to enjoy Eileen's cuisine. The most charming bedrooms are found in the main house, while the rooms in the adjacent cottage appear very crowded together. Orchard has a tiny bathroom ensuite while Bridges and The Oak have private bathrooms across the hall. Of the small rooms in the cottage, Garden is the most appealing, offering a bedside view through low windows across the garden to the sheep at pasture. Apart from lots of country walking, the main attractions of the area are the museums at Ironbridge Gorge which chronicle events during the Industrial Revolution. *Directions:* Take the A49 from Ludlow for 7 miles to Craven Arms, turn right on the B4368 for 4 miles to Diddlebury. Take the first right after the entrance to the village and Glebe Farm is on the left just before the church.

GLEBE FARM
Owners Michael & Eileen Wilkes
Diddlebury
Craven Arms, Shropshire SY7 9DH
Tel: (058476) 221
6 rooms, 5 with private bathrooms
From £20 per person
Open March to October
Children over 8

Drakeston House is an exceptional Cotswold-style home filled with an abundance of lovely antiques. The well-kept grounds invite a leisurely stroll through the tall, clipped hedges laid out by Hugh's grandfather. The interior of Drakeston House has lovely old pine pitch and jarrow wood floors and beamed and plasterwork ceilings, complemented by traditional firebaskets filled with dried flower arrangements and beautiful old furniture. Guests enjoy breakfast round the dining room table where Crystal will, with advance arrangements, also serve dinner for guests' first evening's stay. Upstairs, two bedrooms share the facilities of a large, old-fashioned bathroom which has been modernized. There is also a suite which has an adjoining private bath, a small twin-bedded room suitable for children (crib available), and a larger, double-bedded room that has windows with views both to the side and the front of the house. From Drakeston House you can visit Berkeley Castle and the adjacent Jenner Museum, Slimbridge Wildfowl Trust, Westonbirt Arboretum and, farther afield, Gloucester, Cheltenham, Bath, and Bristol. *Directions:* Northbound travellers leave the M5 at exit 14; southbound at exit 13. Stinchcombe is situated halfway between Dursley and Wotton-under-Edge on the B4060. Drakeston House is signposted on the road.

DRAKESTON HOUSE
Owners Hugh & Crystal St John
Stinchcombe
Dursley, Gloucestershire GL11 6AS
Tel: (0453) 542140
3 rooms, 1 with private bathroom
From £17 per person
Open April to mid-October
Children welcome
No Smoking house
Wolsey Lodge

Julie Graham provides a sincere and relaxed welcome to Ettington Manor and is happy to show guests around her home which has greatly evolved since its original portion was built as a religious establishment in 1267. The drawing room has the comfiest of feather sofas drawn up around an enormous log-burning fireplace. In the adjacent dining room Julie serves dinner by prior arrangement at 7:30 pm. On the night of my visit the menu offered was smoked mackerel pate, leek and potato soup, beef stroganoff, hazelnut meringue with raspberries, and coffee. The bedrooms are simply furnished with new pine furniture and each has a modern, ensuite shower room. If you stay for a week you can rent one of the two holiday cottages. The Chantry sleeps four and has low-beamed ceilings and stud walls. One of the upstairs bedrooms is particularly dramatic, with a four-poster bed sitting center stage in a high-ceilinged room. Next door, The Almshouse is a snug little nest which sleeps three. Ettington Manor is just 6 miles from Stratford-upon-Avon and 10 miles from Warwick Castle. Ragley Hall, Kenilworth, and an abundance of National Trust properties are nearby. *Directions:* Ettington is on the A422 Banbury to Stratford-upon-Avon road. At the center of the village turn south into Rogers Lane and Ettington Manor is the first driveway on your right.

ETTINGTON MANOR
Owner Julie Graham
Ettington
Stratford-upon-Avon, Warwickshire CV37 7SX
Tel: (0789) 740216
4 rooms with private bathrooms
From £25 per person
Open April to October
Credit cards MC, VS
Children over 12
Wolsey Lodge

Over 500 years ago this tiny cottage in this quiet Cotswold village was home to the parish priest and today is a welcoming bed and breakfast. The front door opens into the large guest sitting room where a lovely Welsh dresser holds an array of unusual green and white china and the breakfast room whose massive inglenook fireplace is decorated with country knickknacks. An old lamp hangs over a large round table where guests gather for breakfast, which consists of their choice of traditional bacon and eggs breakfast or smoked haddock and kippers. The free-range eggs come from the next-door farm and honey from Jan's bees. The three guest bedrooms found at the top of the narrow stairs have lots of simple country charm and share the facilities of a large bathroom. A double room has old pine furniture while the twin has roses peeking in at the window and a view across the fields. Husband David, a banker mason, has carved new stone-mullioned windows for the cottage. Exploring the Cotswolds with their rolling hills and pretty villages is most enjoyable but guests also enjoy shopping for clothes and antiques, visiting gardens such as those at Kiftsgate and Hidcote, touring stately homes, and petting the animals in the Cotswold Wildlife Park. *Directions:* Take the Cotswold villages of Chipping Norton, Stow-on-the-Wold and Chipping Campden as a triangle on the map and the small village of Evenlode is at the center of the triangle. Twostones is next to the church.

TWOSTONES
Owners Jan & David Wright
Evenlode
Moreton-in-Marsh, Gloucestershire GL56 0NY
Tel: (0608) 51104
3 rooms sharing 1 bathroom
From £14 per person
Open all year
Children over 10

This one-time farmhouse (parts of it date from the 16th century) is now an unpretentious, well kept bed and breakfast run by Brenda and Ken Webb. Beyond the little bar is a cozy sitting and dining room with chairs drawn round the television, with a large fireplace at one end and a dining area at the other. An adjacent sitting room is more formally furnished with a royal blue velvet sofa and chairs--this is the only room where smoking is permitted. Ken is the resident chef who produces delectable meals. Several bedrooms have nice old beds--while I prefer the old beams and plasterwork of bedrooms in the main house, I much prefer the bathrooms of those in the courtyard addition. Children are very welcome: there is a large grassy garden for them to play in as well as a play yard and play house. Early suppers for children can be provided. Over the Christmas holiday Brenda and Ken offer a four-night festive program that includes a treasure hunt and a visit to the pantomime in addition to holiday parties. Families enjoy visiting Kilverston Wildlife Park and the Bressingham Steam Museum. The Norfolk coast (Cromer is an old-fashioned family seaside resort) and Norwich are a 40-minute drive away. *Directions:* From Diss take the A1066 towards Thetford. After 5 miles turn right to Fersfield, go straight through the village and Strenneth Farmhouse is on your right after 2 miles.

STRENNETH FARMHOUSE
Owners Brenda & Ken Webb
Old Airfield Road
Fersfield, Diss, Norfolk IP22 2BP
Tel: (037988) 8182
9 rooms, 7 with private bathrooms
From £20 per person
Open all year
Credit cards MC, VS
Children welcome

Flamborough is a massive chalk headland jutting out into the North Sea, its tall, white lighthouse flashing a warning to coastal vessels: the sea off Flamborough is the resting place of many ships. The manor was rescued from a derelict state when Lesley moved here with her family. Now chairs and sofas are drawn round the fireplace in the living room whose deep alcoves are filled with books. Across the large hallway the dining room hung with old prints has the feel of a snug country parlor with its rich dark wallpaper, chairs drawn round the fire, needlepoint dining chairs, and a handsome dining table neatly laid for dinner. Guests are encouraged to bring their own wine. An ornate, 17th-century Portuguese bed topped by a thick woolen mattress sits center stage in the principal bedroom which leads to a large well-appointed bathroom. The smaller bedroom has an adjacent bathroom with a splendid claw-foot tub. Jeffrey has revived the craft of knitting ganseys, traditional fishing sweaters, which, along with antiques and needlepoint, are for sale in the shop in the converted stables. To the north lie the picturesque fishing villages of Runswick Bay, Staithes, and Robin Hood's Bay. Inland lies the North Yorkshire Moors National Park. York and Castle Howard are within 44 miles. *Directions:* From Bridlington take the B1255 into Flamborough. Pass St Oswald's church on the right and The Manor House is on the next corner on the right.

THE MANOR HOUSE
Owners Lesley Berry & Jeffrey Miller
Flamborough
Bridlington, Yorkshire YO15 1PD
Tel: (0262) 850943
2 rooms with private bathrooms
From £26.50 per person
Closed Christmas
Children over 8
Wolsey Lodge

Sitting beside the village green at the heart of this quiet, unspoilt Cotswold village, The Lamb is a picture-perfect hostelry. Locals gather in the evening in the quaint bar where pride of place is given to a picture gallery of guide dogs for the blind who have been sponsored by patrons' donations. Decked out in pine, the restaurant with its soft pink decor is most attractive. The menu is a la carte with such dishes as Beef Wellington and grilled lamb cutlets with onion sauce. Simpler fare is served in the bar and adjacent buttery. Up the narrow, winding staircase and down twisting, narrow corridors are an array of picture-perfect, cottage-style bedrooms, all furnished differently (suitable only for the nimble of foot). Two have intricately carved four-poster beds made by Richard. Families often take the two twin bedrooms which share a bathroom. Thick stone walls with deeply set windows, low ceilings, quaint doors, and beams all add to the old-world feel. Two additional rooms are in the converted stable. Outside is a landscaped garden--the perfect place to enjoy a glass of real ale on a warm summer evening--and a heated indoor swimming pool. Most people come here to tour the picturesque Cotswold villages, explore gardens such as Hidcote, and visit Stratford-upon-Avon and Oxford. *Directions:* From the A429 turn into Bourton-on-the-Water, carry on on this road (not into the village) and take the first turn right to Great Rissington.

THE LAMB INN
Owners Kate & Richard Cleverly
Great Rissington
Bourton-on-the-Water, Gloucestershire GL54 2LD
Tel: (0451) 20388
11 rooms, 9 with private bathrooms
From £36 to £50 double
Closed Christmas
Credit cards MC, VS
Children welcome

There are many good reasons to visit Leicestershire and this exceptional home at the edge of a peaceful village with many picturesque thatched cottages is one of them. Here old furniture is gleamingly polished, the windows sparkle, and everything is in apple-pie order. The evening sun streams into the drawing room and books on stately homes and castles invite browsing. Breakfast is served in a small dining room with a long trestle table. If there are several people for dinner, Raili (who grew up in Finland) sets the elegant table in the large dining room, serving a variety of meals using organic vegetables from her garden. The principal bedroom has ensuite facilities, while the other three guest rooms share a large family bathroom. Bedrooms have televisions and someone is always on hand to make a pot of tea. A three-day Christmas program gives guests the opportunity to experience a quiet, traditional English country Christmas--visits to the hunt and the midnight carol service are highlights. Nearby are a great many stately homes (Althorp, Princess Di's family home, Burghley House, and Rockingham Castle, for instance), lots of antique shops, the vast expanse of Rutland Water, cathedrals at Ely and Peterborough, historic towns (Stamford and Uppingham), and ancient villages. *Directions:* From Uppingham take the A47 and turn left at East Norton following signs for the village of Hallaton. Drive through the village and The Old Rectory is next to the church.

THE OLD RECTORY
Owners Raili & Tom Fraser
Hallaton
Market Harborough, Leicestershire LE16 8TY
Tel: (085889) 350
4 rooms, 1 with private bathroom
From £21.50 per person
Open all year
Children over 7

Situated in 10 acres of garden and pasture, Halstock Mill, built in the 17th century, was a working mill until 1937. Since then it has been converted into a lovely country house with oak beams in abundance and a cheerful log fire blazing in the drawing room on the occasional cool summer evening. The dining room, charmingly decorated with blue and white pottery, looks onto the attractive, secluded garden. Jane and Peter Spender pride themselves on serving home-grown or local produce. A typical evening menu consists of onion tart, local river trout with vegetables gathered in the kitchen garden that afternoon, followed by a variety of homemade fruit ices. For breakfast there is a choice of six different cooked dishes (chosen the evening before). All the bedrooms have a tea and coffee tray, television, and a modern bathroom. One bedroom sports a four-poster bed. Halstock Mill is situated in the heart of Thomas Hardy country--perfect for a tranquil holiday, with many historic villages, gardens, churches, and houses within very easy reach. *Directions:* From Yeovil take the A37 for 2 miles and turn right to Halstock (5 miles) where you follow signs for Chedington and after half a mile turn right to Halstock Mill.

HALSTOCK MILL
Owners Jane & Peter Spender
Halstock
Dorset BA22 9SJ
Tel: (093589) 278
4 rooms with private bathrooms
From £20 per person
Closed December & January
Credit cards MC, VS
Children over 8

No longer a farm, this 17th-century house is the adorable home of Mike and Sheila Edwards. Chintz-covered chairs on an oriental carpet, mullioned windows set into thick walls, blackened beams, an antique dresser displaying china, and an old polished table set before a blazing fire in the inglenook fireplace set the picture of coziness that awaits you at Ford Farm House. Upstairs guests have a comfortable sitting room with lots of games, a TV, tea and coffee tray, and biscuits. The bedrooms are particularly inviting: Louise's Room is a sunny single with lots of books, the Patchwork Room has a patchwork quilt on its double bed and a private bathroom, and the Flower Room has watercolor prints of flowers, flowery curtains, and shares a large bathroom with Louise's Room. If you are looking for self-catering accommodation, the Edwards can offer two adorable little cottages across the courtyard. A delicious breakfast is the only meal served: for dinner guests usually walk down the quiet village lanes to the nearby Church House Inn. Harberton is well placed for exploring Devon: historic Totnes with its castle, Elizabethan Dartmouth with its naval college, picturesque Salcombe, Buckfastleigh with its abbey, and the wild expanses of Dartmoor National Park. *Directions:* Take the A38 round Exeter, then the A384 to Totnes where you take the A381 Kingsbridge road to your right on the outskirts of town. After 2 miles turn right to Harberton and Ford Farm is the first old house in the village.

FORD FARM HOUSE
Owners Mike & Sheila Edwards
Harberton
Totnes, Devon TQ9 7JS
Tel: (0803) 863539
3 rooms, 1 with private bathroom
From £17 per person
Open all year
Children over 12

Christine and David Cooper have lovingly and with great imagination converted this 17th-century mill into a secluded hideaway. The Dutch door entrance leads into a spacious lounge with two round stone grinding stones on the floor and antique pulleys and gears above. From here separate steep, narrow staircases lead up to two tiny bedrooms tucked under the eaves. Although small, each bedroom is bright and cheery with sun streaming in from the overhead skylight. Christine has prettily decorated each with matching curtains, bedspreads, and cushions. The bathrooms are reached by very steep, ladder-like steps down from the bedroom (making this definitely not a place to stay for the infirm). Work is under way to provide two more rooms in the very old granary. Breakfast is served in the Coopers' cottage connected to the mill by a passage reached through a trap door in the parlor. Dinner is not served but a bountiful supper tray can be ordered. This is the area where A. A. Milne lived and wrote about his son, Christopher Robin, and his teddy bear, Winnie the Pooh, playing in Ashdown Forest. Christine has a walking map to lead you to all their enchanted places. *Directions:* Take the A264 from Tunbridge Wells, then go 1 mile south on the B2026 towards Hartfield. Turn left just past Perryhill Nurseries on the unpaved road and follow the B & B signs.

BOLEBROKE MILL
Owners Christine & David Cooper
Edenbridge Road
Hartfield, Sussex TN7 4JP
Tel: (0892) 770425
2 rooms with private bathrooms
From £20 per person
Credit cards AX, VS
Open March to October
Children over 7
No Smoking house

It was love at first sight when I came upon Carr Head Farm sitting high above Hathersage village with steep crags and windswept heather moors as a backdrop. The garden presents a large flagstone patio, a profusion of flowers nestled in little niches in the terraces leading down to a sweeping lawn, and the most spectacular view across this beautiful Derbyshire valley. The beauty of Mary Barber's gardens is matched by the loveliness of her home where everything has been done with caring and impeccable taste. The beamed dining room is furnished in period style with groupings of tables and chairs where guests gather for breakfast, the only meal served. The adjacent drawing room is very elegant in blues and creams, a bowl of sweets sitting on the coffee table next to a stack of interesting books. The three lovely bedrooms share the facilities of a bathroom with shower upstairs and another downstairs. The four-poster room offers beautiful views of the valley. The Peak District with its picturesque villages, stone-walled fields, and dramatic dales is on your doorstep, as are Haddon Hall and Chatsworth House. *Directions:* Exit the M1 at junction 29 towards Baslow where you take the A623 to the B6001, through Grindleford, towards Castleton. At the junction with the main road, turn right, turn left on School Lane, and then just before the church (Little John of Robin Hood fame has his grave in the churchyard) turn right up Church Bank to the farm.

CARR HEAD FARM
Owner Mary Barber
Church Bank
Hathersage
Sheffield, Yorkshire S30 1BR
Tel: (0433) 50383
3 rooms sharing 2 bathrooms
From £13.50 per person
Closed Christmas
Children over 12

The only hint in this most English of country houses that Bob and Eeke van Gulik hail from Holland is the pair of clogs sitting beside the front door. After many years travelling abroad, Bob has turned his hand to his one-time hobby cooking, while Eeke assists him in the kitchen and makes guests welcome. Their aim is to create a convivial house-party atmosphere (though guests do dine at individual tables) and their desire is to get to know their visitors and to share their love of the area with them. They discourage (and charge a supplement for) one-night stays and guests are expected to dine in except on Tuesdays. Maps and information on the many walks and sights of this lovely area are spread across the grand piano in the dining room. Two snug lounges are there for guests to use. Guests are introduced to one another and often enjoy chatting together, but can always retire to the second lounge for privacy. They accept children but like to confirm by phone that parents are in charge of their children at all times as they find that most of their guests are in search of a quiet country break. The bedrooms vary in size, the larger rooms having a single as well as a double bed. There are many good walks from the house and Hill Top, the Lakeland home of Beatrix Potter, is nearby. *Directions:* From Ambleside take the A593 towards Coniston and after a mile turn left on the B5286 towards Hawkshead. Half a mile past the Outgate Inn turn right at the sign for Field Head. The house is the second drive on the right

FIELD HEAD HOUSE
Owners Eeke & Bob van Gulik
Hawkshead, Cumbria LA22 0PY
Tel: (09666) 240
7 rooms with private bathrooms
From £29 per person
Open all year
Phone regarding children
Wolsey Lodge

Sheltered in a gentle fold of the hills beneath the spectacular crags of Haytor Rocks, Haytor Vale is a quiet village containing little cottages and the Rock Inn. With its wooden beams and huge open fireplace, the inn has a cozy, traditional ambience. Bedrooms are named after horses that have won the Grand National: Lovely has an old oak four-poster bed and a dark beamed ceiling, Master Robert and Freeboooter are rooms with sloping ceilings and large private bathrooms. A relatively small supplement is charged for these deluxe rooms, and it is well worth paying. All the bedrooms have television (including a movie channel), tea and coffee, telephone, and a mini bar. The food here is delightful: bar meals range from traditional roasts to curries (the desserts are especially tempting), while the candlelit restaurant serves a set-price dinner with a wide variety of choices for each course. From the giant rocky outcrop of neighboring Haytor Rocks you can see the vast extent of Dartmoor National Park, the Teign estuary, and rolling hills of southern Devon. The nearby quarry supplied the stone used for building London Bridge, which now resides in America. *Directions:* Take the M5 from Exeter which joins the A38, Plymouth road, then the A382 to Bovey Tracey. At the first roundabout turn left and follow the road up to Haytor and cross a cattle grid onto the moor. After passing an old petrol station, turn left into Haytor Vale.

THE ROCK INN
Owner Christopher Graves
Haytor Vale
Newton Abbot, Devon TQ13 9XP
Tel: (0364) 661305 fax: (0364) 661242
10 rooms, 8 with private bathrooms
From £26 per person
Open all year
Credit cards all major
Children welcome

Henley-on-Thames, a bustling town known for its regatta, is located only a half hour's drive from Heathrow International Airport. On its outskirts lies Shepherds Green, a collection of homes gathered around a lawn. Shepherds bed and breakfast is surrounded by trim lawns and an orchard where a goat grazes. It appears to be a substantial 1930s home with scented vines growing up to its large mullioned windows, an appearance which belies the age of its core, which actually dates from the 16th century. The low-beamed ceiling in the dining room and the long refectory table evoke the old origins of the house. In the spacious sitting room there is ample space for a grouping of sofas and chairs around the fireplace, a grand piano, and some fine pieces of antique furniture. Bedrooms are very pleasantly furnished; the very large double has a large ensuite bathroom, the family room has a sitting area in the bay window, and the small single is used mainly for children. For dinner, guests often eat at a country pub (The Dog and Duck near Nettlebed or The Grouse and Claret on Sonning Common) or dine at one of the many restaurants in Henley. From Henley to Windsor is a very lovely stretch of the River Thames which winds through Hurley, Marlow, and Cookham to Boulters Lock and on to Bray and Windsor with its magnificent castle. *Directions:* Cross the bridge into Henley, go through the town, up the hill, and after 3 miles turn right to Shepherds Green. Shepherds is signposted on the right.

SHEPHERDS
Owner Susan Fulford-Dobson
Shepherds Green, Rotherfield Greys
Henley-on-Thames, Oxfordshire RG9 4QL
Tel: (04917) 413
3 rooms, 2 with private bathrooms
From £21 per person
Closed Christmas
Children over 12

This timbered, pink house and its black-painted wooden barn hug a quiet country road on the edge of the peaceful Suffolk village of Higham. Meg Parker, with her gentle dalmatian Percy at her heels, offers a warm smile and a sincere welcome to her home, quickly putting visitors at ease. Meg leads her guests to the lovely drawing room and then escorts them up the broad staircase to their rooms. Breakfast is enjoyed around the large dining room table, and, since it is the only meal served, she is happy to offer advice on where to dine, often suggesting The Angel at Stoke by Nayland. Bedrooms vary in size from large twin-bedded rooms to a cozy double room, in the oldest part of the house, with an ensuite bathroom. Outside, Meg's large garden is carefully tended and stretches towards the River Brett where a rowing boat is available for guests' use. The narrow Brett soon becomes the broader Stour and you can row upstream for a picnic and idly drift home or go downstream to Stratford St Mary and work off a lunch at The Swan by rowing back upstream. An unheated swimming pool is tucked into one sheltered corner of the garden and a well-kept tennis court occupies another. A highlight of a stay here is to visit Flatford, immortalized in the paintings of John Constable. *Directions:* Leave the A12 between Colchester and Ipswich at Stratford St Mary. The Old Vicarage is 1 mile to the west next to the church.

THE OLD VICARAGE
Owners Meg & John Parker
Higham
Colchester, Suffolk CO7 6JY
Tel: (020) 637248
4 rooms, 2 with private bathrooms
From £20 per person
Open all year
Children welcome
Wolsey Lodge

The outstanding feature of The Old Rectory is the bedrooms, their decor and furnishings being superior to those offered in many expensive country house hotels. Clun Suite offers a very large bedroom, bathroom, and adjacent sitting room. Shropshire is decked out in many coordinating shades of green complemented by light wood furniture. Kerry, though smaller and plainer, is still a favorite due to its sparkling modern bathroom and large expanse of windows that stretch almost from ceiling to floor, framing a spectacular view of the garden and nearby fields which you can enjoy from two comfortable armchairs. Bookcases are packed with novels in the upstairs hallway while downstairs in the guest drawing room maps and where-to-go books fill another bookcase. French windows open up to Graham's garden, and he is happy to wax lyrical on his trees, bushes and flowers. Amy cooks a variety of delicious dinners and is always happy to offer a vegetarian alternative. Apart from peace, quiet and country walks, the main attractions of the area are Stokesay Castle, Ludlow, Shrewsbury, and the Ironbridge Gorge museums. *Directions:* Take the A49 from Ludlow for 7 miles to Craven Arms then turn left on the B4368 signposted Clun. At Aston-on-Clun turn right over the small bridge by The Flag Tree (literally a tree festooned in flags) for Hopesay (1 mile) and The Old Rectory is on the left next to the church.

THE OLD RECTORY
Owners Graham & Amy Spencer
Hopesay
Craven Arms, Shropshire SY7 8HD
Tel: (05887) 245
3 rooms with private bathrooms
From £23 per person
Closed Christmas
Children over 12
Wolsey Lodge

Set in a valley carved by a stream rushing down from high, bleak moorlands, Hutton-le-Hole is a cluster of pale stone houses, a picturesque village in the heart of the spectacular North Yorkshire Moors National Park. The lintel above the Hammer and Hand's doorway declares the date of the house, built as a beer house for the iron workers, as 1784. Now it is home to Alison, formerly a lawyer, and John, once a London policeman, and their young son Giles who happily welcome guests to their bed and breakfast. John's passion for cricket explains the old cricket prints hanging in the sitting and dining rooms. Tucked behind the dining room (dinner is available on request) is a minute bar offering just enough room for a drink before dinner. A blazing log fire crackles in the large hearth in the sitting room, a warm spot to toast one's toes. A narrow staircase leads to three tiny bedrooms, each prettily decorated to give a feeling of light and warmth. Hutton-le-Hole houses the Ryedale Folk Museum which is well worth a visit. Walking is a great attraction hereabouts, though a less strenuous way to see the park is aboard the nostalgic steam train that runs from Pickering. York with its many attractions is less than an hour's drive away and Castle Howard is even closer. *Directions:* Take the A170 from Thirsk towards Pickering. The left-hand turn to Hutton-le-Hole is signposted just after Kirbymoorside. The Hammer and Hand is at the heart of the village next to the Crown Inn.

HAMMER & HAND GUEST HOUSE
Owners Alison & John Wilkins
Hutton-le-Hole
York, Yorkshire YO6 6UA
Tel: (07515) 300
3 rooms with private bathrooms
From £22 per person
Closed Christmas
Children welcome

Caldrees Manor is a lovely old home, a rambling manor house with additions built over the years to accommodate a large family with many servants. Kerry and Bevan Braithwaite have put their large home to work for them as a dinner, bed and breakfast, with guests occupying the extremely comfortable bedrooms that are surplus to the family's needs. While this is a very grand home, everything about it is very relaxed and decidedly unstuffy. The sitting room's gray marble fireplace is flanked by soft white brocade sofas in front of which an old marching band drum serves as a coffee table. High windows look out over spacious lawns that lead down to a small lake where ducks swim. The snug library has a leather sofa and chairs cozily drawn around the fireplace. An ornately carved golden oak staircase with a winged dragon on the newel post leads up to the bedrooms whose pretty decor gives a light, airy feeling. Each is named after its predominant color: The Blue Room is a particularly large room with stairs leading up to the bathroom. Close by is Cambridge, a historic college and town best explored on foot, though taking a boat or punt is a romantic way to enjoy the River Cam. *Directions:* If travelling from the north, leave the M11 at exit 10, if travelling from the south, leave at exit 9. Caldrees Manor is in the center of the village of Ickleton, opposite the Red Lion pub.

CALDREES MANOR
Owners Kerry & Bevan Braithwaite
Ickleton
Saffron Waldon, Essex CB10 1S5
Tel: (0799) 30253
4 rooms with private bathrooms
From £30 per person
Open all year
Children welcome
Wolsey Lodge

There are many good reasons to visit the Yorkshire Dales and this exceptional home near the romantic ruins of Jervaulx Abbey is one of them. From the moment I entered I was captivated by the enviable antiques and country collectibles that fill every nook and cranny. Everywhere you look you find glassware, hatpins, family pictures, and china, all as artfully arranged as the flowers that grace every room. A long, low bench groaning with books and magazines sits before the open fireplace in the drawing room, needlepoint cushions are scattered on the sofa, and comfy chairs are drawn round. It is here that Angela, Ian, and their guests gather in the evening after dinner to "put the world to rights." The kitchen is the heart of the house: guest pop in for a chat and children eat an early supper at the enormous pine table before the old blackened range and bread ovens while Angela prepares dinner served at the large dining room table. The bedrooms are all a delight and, of course, filled with antiques. There is also a self-catering apartment, rented by the week, which is furnished to the same high standard as the house and has a lock-off arrangement whereby it can be either one- or two-bedroom accommodation. The Old Hall is set on the edge of the Yorkshire Dales, convenient for exploring York and Harrogate. *Directions:* Jervaulx Abbey is 15 miles west of Ripon on the A6108, half-way between Masham and Leyburn.

THE OLD HALL
Owners Angela & Ian Close
Jervaulx Abbey
Ripon, Yorkshire HG4 4PH
Tel: (0677) 60313
3 rooms with private bathrooms
From £28 per person
Open all year
Children welcome
Wolsey Lodge

Once in a while we discover an inn so enticing that we just want to unpack our bags and settle in. Meadow House is definitely such a place. It was with great reluctance that we departed from this exquisite Georgian manor, originally a 16th-century rectory but now owned by a warmly gracious couple, the Samsons. The setting is utter tranquility: the house is surrounded by countryside with 8 acres of gardens including a duck pond, small stream, meadows, woods, and farmland. The coast is just a few minutes' walk from the house, and offers bluffs for strolling and a rocky beach for fossil hunting. Back at the manor, guests can relax in the study or the drawing room in front of a cheery fire, or perhaps play a game of billiards. The bedrooms are especially spacious, fresh, and decorated with elegant taste. All are very pretty but my favorite is room 2, which is a cheery corner room with a happy yellow motif. Each room contains pampering touches such as a hair dryer, fresh flowers, tea and coffee selections, cookies, color TV, and direct dial telephone. There are also additional rooms tucked into the converted stables. Wine aficionados will appreciate the Meadow House's award-winning wine cellar. This is truly an idyllic haven for those who love the sea and seclusion. *Directions:* Arriving from Bridgwater on the A39, turn right in Kilve just before the Hood Arms pub onto Sea Lane. Meadow House is 1/2 mile on the left.

MEADOW HOUSE
Owners Alec & Tina Samson
Sea Lane
Kilve, Somerset TA5 1EG
Tel: (027874) 546
4 rooms & 4 cottages with private bathrooms
From £51 single & £74 double
Closed Christmas
Credit cards all major
Children over 9

The magnificent scenery of the Lake District, the Yorkshire Dales, and Hadrian's Wall are within easy driving distance of Hipping Hall, so visitors can easily justify a stay of several days in Jocelyn Ruffle and Ian Bryant's comfortable home. Guests help themselves to pre-dinner drinks from the honesty bar in the conservatory which links the main part of the house to the Great Hall where dinner is served. A soaring, beamed ceiling and a broad oak-plank floor provide an impressive setting for the excellent five-course meal served around one large table where guests are looked after by Ian while Jos creates in the kitchen. Ian selects wine to complement each course. The bedrooms are named after local hills and dales, and all are comfortably and very tastefully furnished, often with lovely old pieces bought at local auctions. Each has its own sparkling new, well-equipped bathroom. The 4 acres of garden are a delight and feature a large expanse of lawn set up for croquet and a kitchen garden which provides many of the vegetables enjoyed at dinner. Two suites, named Emily and Charlotte after the Bronte sisters who attended school in Cowan Bridge, occupy a courtyard cottage. They each have a kitchen and living room downstairs, bedroom and bathroom upstairs. *Directions:* Leave the M6 at junction 36 and follow the A65 through Kirkby Lonsdale towards Skipton. Hipping Hall is on the left, 3 miles after leaving Kirkby Lonsdale.

HIPPING HALL
Owners Jocelyn Ruffle & Ian Bryant
Cowan Bridge
Kirkby Lonsdale, Cumbria LA6 2JJ
Tel: (05242) 71187
5 rooms with private bathrooms (+2 suites)
From £29 per person
Open March to first week in November
Credit cards MC, VS
Children over 12

Prospect Hill Hotel has a serene, "end of the earth" feel to it, though it is only 9 miles from the M6 motorway. Just outside the picturesque village of Kirkoswald, John and Isa Henderson have creatively restored this 18th-century farmhouse and outbuildings, converting them into a delightfully original country hotel. John's collection of old farm implements in the courtyard sets a country mood which is felt throughout the hotel. The bar was the cow byre and the dining room the hay barn, featuring a lofty, intricate, oak-timbered ceiling. The bedrooms, varying in size, are all decorated with simple, country-style furnishings and reflect the unpretentious style of the hotel. Only five bedrooms have private bathrooms, and, of these, Woodend and Park View have lovely antique brass beds. Several rooms are located across the courtyard in the annex. All the rooms have an information book on interesting walks and the local area. The Lake District and Hadrian's Wall are both easily visited from Kirkoswald. *Directions:* If approaching from the south, leave the M6 at junction 41 onto the A6 to Plumpton, turn right onto B6413 through Lazonby and Kirkoswald, then straight on and up a steep hill and the hotel is on your left after half a mile.

PROSPECT HILL HOTEL
Owners Isa & John Henderson
Kirkoswald
Penrith, Cumbria CA10 1ER
Tel: (076883) 500
9 rooms, 5 with private bathrooms
From £21 single to £55 double
Closed Christmas
Credit cards all major
Children welcome

Lacock was once a prosperous medieval wool town and now it is preserved by the National Trust as one of the most picturesque of British villages--its streets lined with splendid old houses and cottages. Next to the church, King John's Hunting Lodge is an olde-English tea shop serving thick slices of homemade fruit cake and fluffy scones topped with Jersey cream as accompaniments to piping hot pots of tea. Fortunately for visitors, the lodge offers two simple bedrooms sharing the facilities of one bathroom. The large front bedroom has a delightful old four-poster bed and a romantic window seat, while the adjoining dressing room has two single beds suitable for children. Next door the very prettily decorated Church Room overlooks the churchyard. There are three quaint pubs in the village that do evening meals, or, if you prefer, a magnificent, candlelit five-course banquet is offered by At The Sign of The Angel--an adorable black and white timbered inn just down the street. A short stroll away is Lacock Abbey. This abbey was converted from a religious establishment to a mansion in the 16th century but still retains its 13th-century cloisters. The barn houses a display of Henry Fox Talbot's early photographs, apparatus, and letters. *Directions:* Leave the M4 at junction 17 and take the A350 Melksham road south to Lacock.

KING JOHN'S HUNTING LODGE
Owners Bob & Jane Woods
21 Church Street
Lacock
Wiltshire SN15 2LB
Tel: (0249) 730313
2 rooms sharing 1 bathroom
From £18 per person
Closed Christmas
Children welcome

The Farmhouse Hotel and Restaurant is very much a Rouse family operation: Dad (Don) runs the dairy farm, Mum (Mary) operates the farmhouse as a hotel, son Wesley is the hotel manager, and daughter Julia the chef. Surrounded by its outbuildings and facing a large garden, this 17th-century Cotswold stone farmhouse has been tastefully converted while retaining the cozy charm of its walk-in fireplaces, oak beams, and low ceilings. Bedrooms are named after Oxford colleges and range from small attic rooms with dormer windows (Trinity and Keebles) to a luxurious double where the soft pink color of the walls and carpet is picked up in the flower-sprigged drapes, ornate bedhead, and drapes (Queens). Nuffield is a ground-floor room equipped for the handicapped. The restaurant has been extended from the beamed farmhouse dining room into a Victorian-style conservatory. Dinner begins with hors d'oeuvres followed by soup and sorbet. The main course is a choice of one of two meats from the carvery or two specials. University Farm is a very informal place; I know of no other hotel where guests can ask to visit the cows being milked. Oxford and Woodstock are just a short drive away. *Directions:* University Farm is on the A4095 (Faringdon road) 3 miles south of Witney. Unfortunately, RAF Brize Norton is nearby, so be prepared for some aircraft noise.

THE FARMHOUSE HOTEL & RESTAURANT
Owners The Rouse Family
University Farm, Lew
Bampton, Oxfordshire OX8 2AU
Tel: (0993) 850297
6 rooms with private bathrooms
From £23 per person
Closed Christmas
Credit cards MC, VS
Children over 5

Tucked in an unspoiled valley high above the hustle and bustle of the more well-known Lake District tourist routes, this traditional pub lies surrounded by the ruggedly beautiful Lakeland scenery. Built of somber-looking slate in 1872 as a resting place for travellers, the hostelry is still a base for tourists, many of whom come here for the walking. They gather by the bar, the sound of their hiking boots echoing hollowly against the slate floor, poring over maps and discussing the day's activities. By contrast, the carpeted and curtained dining room and lounge with its velour chairs seem very sedate. The Stephenson family pride themselves on the quality of their food and offer a five-course meal in addition to substantial bar meals. Do not expect grand things of the accommodations as this is not a luxury establishment. But, for travellers who enjoy quietly decorated, simply furnished, and spotlessly clean rooms with modern bathrooms, the Three Shires fills the bill. Just a few miles away are some of the Lake District's most popular villages: Hawkshead, Ambleside, Coniston, and Grasmere. *Directions:* From Ambleside take the A593, Coniston road, cross Skelwith Bridge, and take the first right, signposted The Langdales and Wrynose Pass. Take the first left to Little Langdale and the Three Shires Inn is on your right.

THREE SHIRES INN
Owners The Stephenson Family
Little Langdale
Ambleside, Cumbria LA22 9N2
Tel: (09667) 215
11 rooms, 7 with private bathrooms
From £24 per person
Open February to November & New Years
Children welcome

Little Rissington Manor is a wonderful find, a Victorian mansion set in 11 acres of grounds including vast lawns sweeping down from the house to a tennis court and a swimming pool. Annabel Kirkpatrick, her two vivacious young daughters, Lucy and Sophie, along with the friendly family dogs welcome you to their home. The elegant drawing and dining rooms are not for guests' use but there is a small cozy room with a fire, TV, and lots of tourist literature. At the top of the grand staircase, guests have the exclusive use of the bedrooms at the front of the house. There are five bedrooms, but Annabel takes only six guests at a time so that she can tailor the rooms' occupancy to guests' demands for singles without charging a supplement. The two choicest rooms are the enormous master bedrooms that occupy the front of the house. Both of these fine rooms have an ensuite bathroom, and the double has an interlinking single that makes a perfect suite of rooms for a family. A traditional English breakfast is served in the small room adjoining the kitchen. Annabel enjoys recommending interesting little pubs in "less touristy" villages for dining. Bourton-on-the-Water, one of the most delightful villages in the Cotswolds, lies a scant mile and half away. *Directions:* From the A429 turn into Bourton-on-the-Water and continue on this road (not into the village) to Little Rissington, where the Manor is on the left just at the entrance to the village.

LITTLE RISSINGTON MANOR
Owner Annabel Kirkpatrick
Little Rissington
Bourton-on-the-Water, Gloucestershire GL54 2NB
Tel: (0451) 21078
5 rooms, 2 with private bathrooms
From £18 per person
Open March to September/October
Children welcome
No Smoking house

Neil and Judy Burns-Thomson came to the wide, flat vistas of Norfolk so that Neil could start a landscaping and garden maintenance company; his first project was to plant the verges of their long driveway with saplings. They have an easy, friendly way about them that makes guests feel right at home and life is very informal here. The Burns-Thomsons share pre-dinner drinks with guests in the sitting room, dine with them in the flagstone dining room at the large trestle table, and enjoy conversations afterwards over coffee. Dating from Tudor times, the house has lots of charming features such as exposed beams and low, sometimes sloping ceilings. Neil and Judy have cleverly removed the plasterwork between two rooms to make a spacious sitting room with the old wooden supports intact as a decorative partition between seating areas. The two double bedrooms at the top of the steep, narrow staircase are cottage-cozy, yet spacious, and have exposed beams and white plasterwork. Pretty floral fabrics adorn the bedspreads and matching curtains. It is a short drive into Norwich to view its splendid 12th-century keep, now the Castle Museum, and to visit Norwich Cathedral. Between Norwich and the holiday resort of Great Yarmouth lie the Norfolk Broads, full of birdlife and boating enthusiasts. *Directions:* Long Stratton is 10 miles south of Norwich on the A140. Turn left past the church into Hall Lane and Mayfield Farm is on the right after a mile.

MAYFIELD FARM
Owners Judy & Neil Burns-Thomson
Long Stratton
Norwich, Norfolk NR15 2RX
Tel: (0508) 31763
2 rooms sharing 1 bathroom
£25 per person
Closed Christmas
Children over 12
Wolsey Lodge

The Moat House is a tall black and white Tudor home with a narrow footbridge leading across a little moat and old cannons whimsically guarding its ancient doorway. The sitting room has dark oak paneling and mullioned windows overlooking the paddock and the beamed dining room has clusters of farmhouse tables and chairs. Old wooden latch doors click softly to reveal the bedrooms with gorgeous half-tester beds, each intricately draped with soft fabrics. Shower rooms are ensuite but if guests prefer to luxuriate in an elegant Victorian claw-foot bathtub, they can use the bathroom across the hall. A low lintel door leads to the large third bedroom, a long room that spans the width of the house, which has a brass and iron double and single bed, tiny windows set in the beamed walls, and a spacious bathroom. Ducks waddle slowly across the lawn, rare breeds of sheep graze in the pasture, and the stables are filled with statuesque horses. Being just a few miles from the M5 and M50 motorways means that guests can easily use The Moat House as a base for explorations into Wales, the Cotswolds, and the like. *Directions:* From Tewkesbury take the A38 in the direction of Worcester for 3/4 of a mile, then turn left on the A438 towards Ledbury for 2 1/2 miles. At Long Green turn right on the B4211 to Longdon and The Moat House is the first house on the left when entering the village.

THE MOAT HOUSE
Owners Sue Virr & Brendan Patterson
Longdon
Tewkesbury, Gloucestershire GL20 6AT
Tel: (068 481) 313
3 rooms with private bathrooms
From £22 per person
Closed Christmas
Children over 6
No Smoking house

When the Richards bought this house they were unaware that their cottage-style home with its maze of little rooms was in fact a medieval great hall with giant wooden beams and roof trusses. Careful restoration has revealed the large parlor below and the great hall above. While the parlor with its mullioned windows, beamed ceiling, and sofas arranged before the huge stone fireplace causes guests to "ooh and aah," it is the great hall that makes them gasp as they regard the massive roof trusses and the maze of intricate timberwork soaring overhead. The soft glow of flickering candlelight bathes guests as they dine at the refectory table in the great hall. Cozy, beamed bedrooms are decorated to perfection in country-print fabrics and have accompanying bathrooms neatly tucked under the rafters. The garden, which is completely encircled by a wide moat, has a willow-shaded fish pond which is home to lazily swimming ducks. Nearby Shrewsbury with its twisting lanes, castle, and open pillared market hall deserves exploration. Farther afield are the Ironbridge Gorge Museum and the historic town of Ludlow. *Directions:* From Shrewsbury take the A49 south for 8 miles: Longnor is signposted to the left. Go through the village past the school and turn left into the lane marked "No Through Road." When the lane turns left Moat House is straight ahead.

MOAT HOUSE
Owners Margaret & Peter Richards
Longnor
Shrewsbury, Shropshire SY5 7PP
Tel: (074373) 434
3 rooms with private bathrooms
From £29 per person
Open March to November
Credit cards MC, VS
No children
Wolsey Lodge

Food is an important part of staying at Feldon House and Allan Witherick has gained quite a reputation for his table, attracting guests from far and wide to his largely Victorian home set in a long, narrow garden next to the village church. Allan decides what he is going to cook for dinner based on which fresh ingredients capture his fancy at the market. Dinner is served either around the large dining room table in the wood-paneled dining room or at small tables in the conservatory. On warm summer evenings drinks and coffee are served on the herringbone brick terrace and the lawn is set for a leisurely game of croquet. The two bedrooms in the main house are prettily decorated and have their bathrooms across the hall. Across the garden a Victorian coach house has been most tastefully converted into additional accommodation. In the upstairs bedroom a grand four-poster bed is topped by a handmade quilt and the downstairs room is decorated in a Chinese motif. These rooms have televisions, tea and coffee trays with fresh biscuits, and sparkling, modern ensuite bathrooms. Stratford-upon-Avon is 15 miles away, while to the south lie the picturesque rolling hills of the Cotswolds with their mellow stone villages and gorgeous gardens such as Hidcote and Kiftsgate. *Directions:* Lower Brailes is on the B4035 between Banbury and Shipston-on-Stour. Feldon House is set back from the main road next to the church.

FELDON HOUSE
Owners Maggie & Allan Witherick
Lower Brailes
Banbury, Oxfordshire OX15 5HW
Tel: (060885) 580
4 rooms with private bathrooms
From £22 per person
Open all year
Credit cards VS
No children

The Salweys of Shropshire can trace their lineage hereabouts back to 1216 and The Lodge has been in their family since it was built in the early 1700s, but it is definitely not a formal place. Guests are likely to find Hermione in her wellies in the garden or dressed in jeans preparing dinner for her guests and family. She puts guests at ease, encouraging them to feel as though they are friends of the family, and enjoys pointing out the architectural details of the house and explaining who's who amongst the family portraits. In the evening, guests gather in the morning room and help themselves to drinks from the honesty bar before going into dinner at a spectacular long table made of burled wood, especially made for the house. Up the grand staircase are four large bedrooms, each with its own private bathroom. The front three bedrooms are the most attractive; Chinese has a suite of furniture painted in an Asian motif, Roses is a large double with an enormous bathroom, and The Yellow Room is a large twin with its bathroom across the hall. The nearest tourist attraction is the medieval town of Ludlow with its old inns, alleyways of antique shops, Norman castle, and riverside walks. *Directions:* Leave Ludlow over Ludford Bridge travelling south. After 1 1/2 miles turn right on the B4361 signposted Richards Castle. After 400 yards turn right through the entrance gates of The Lodge by a curved stone wall, and continue up the long drive to the house.

THE LODGE
Owners Hermione & Humphrey Salwey
Ludlow, Shropshire SY8 4DU
Tel: (0584) 872103
4 rooms with private bathrooms
From £30 per person
Open April to October
No children
Wolsey Lodge

Maiden Newton House is an elegant, honey-colored stone manor house, which, although conveniently located near the center of the small town of Maiden Newton, is kept serenely remote from civilization by 21 acres of lawn and garden. The day we arrived, Bryan Ferriss, the owner, had just returned from the garden with an armful of glorious flowers which he arranged into a dramatic bouquet. His wife, Elizabeth, appeared from the kitchen where she had been supervising the preparations for the evening meal. Elizabeth is renowned for her cooking and dinner is served each night "family-style" at one large table in the elegant dining room overlooking the garden. All meals are prepared with only the freshest of ingredients and most vegetables are homegrown. Fresh fish is frequently served as the main course. A cozy, yet elegant lounge, warmed on chilly days by an open fire, is a favorite gathering place for guests before dinner. Upstairs are six guest rooms, each unique and prettily decorated. It is just a short drive to the lovely Dorset coast. Houses and gardens of interest include Kingston Lacy, Parnham House, Montacute, and Athelhampton. *Directions:* Maiden Newton is on the A356 Dorchester to Crewkerne road. From the center of the village take the A37 Yeovil road. Maiden Newton House is just behind the church.

MAIDEN NEWTON HOUSE
Owners Elizabeth and Bryan Ferriss
Maiden Newton
Dorchester, Dorset DT2 OAA
Tel: (0300) 20336
6 rooms with private bathrooms
From £74 per person dinner, B&B
Closed January to mid-February
Credit cards MC, VS
Children welcome, under 12s served an early supper
Wolsey Lodge

For centuries Barracott farm has been tucked in a gentle hillside overlooking Hayne Down and Hound Tor at the heart of Dartmoor. This wild and beautiful area is now a national park and Barracott the home of Val and Jim Lee. Guests enter this stone house via the alpine garden and through a Dutch door into the broad hallway and cozy guests' sitting room where guests are served a spectacular, mouth-watering, multi-course breakfast including homemade yogurt and fresh-baked bread. From the sitting room, a doorway opens to a little staircase which leads up to the two cottage-style bedrooms, simply decorated with matching drapes and bedspreads. For dinner you are directed to The Kestor in Manaton or the Rock Inn in Haytor Vale. Falling under the spell of this lovely spot, visitors often walk Easdon Moor, which rises behind Barracott, to explore its hut circles which are the ancient foundations of Bronze Age homes. The wild beauty of Dartmoor with its sheltered villages and market towns has a magic all its own; deep valleys, rushing streams, and wild moorlands crowned by rock formations. Buckfast and Buckland Abbeys, National Trust properties such as Castle Drago, the Devonshire coast, and Cornwall are among the sightseeing possibilities. *Directions:* From Exeter take the A38 to the A382, Bovey Tracy, turnoff. At the second roundabout turn left following signs for Manaton. Go through Manaton, and, beyond the village, turn left at the T-junction and then take the first right to Barracott.

BARRACOTT
Owners Val & Jim Lee
Manaton
Newton Abbot, Devon TQ13 9XA
Tel: (0647) 22312
2 rooms with private bathrooms
From £18.50 per person
Open April to October
Children welcome if family takes both rooms

Wigham looks like a picture-perfect postcard of a thatched farmhouse with a sunny terrace and lovely flower garden in front. Steps lead down to a small, fence-enclosed swimming pool. The large beamed dining room is cozily inviting, with a long refectory table strategically set before the massive open hearth. The dining room leads into the sitting room, an inviting room with a large open fireplace dominating one wall and the opposite wall covered by an enormous mural depicting Cromwell sitting upon his horse as his entourage passed before Wigham. A billiard lounge completes the guest living areas. Up the main staircase are three large, extremely comfortable guest bedrooms, each with an especially spacious, beautifully equipped bathroom. My favorite bedroom was The Grey Room, appealingly decorated in pinks and grays and with large windows overlooking the beautiful rolling hills. Two additional bedrooms are above the small parlor. Thirty acres of rich farmland surround the house and provide ingredients for excellent, farm-fresh meals. There are many historic houses and ancient monuments within a short distance, as are Dartmoor and Exmoor. *Directions:* From Exeter take the A377 through Crediton to Morchard Bishop where you turn downhill towards Chawleigh and Chumleigh for under a mile. Fork right by the post box in the wall and after a mile turn right on a narrow lane signposted Wigham.

WIGHAM
Owners Lesley & Stephen Chilcott
Morchard Bishop
Crediton, Devon EX17 6RJ
Tel: (03637) 350
5 rooms with private bathrooms
From £44 per person dinner, B&B
Open all year
Children over 10
No Smoking house

Mungrisdale is one of the few unspoilt villages left in the Lake District and is made up of a pub, an old church, and a cluster of houses and farms set at the foot of rugged, gray-blue crags. Do not confuse The Mill with the adjoining pub of the same name; park next to the pub and walk through the adjacent garden to arrive at this cozy hotel. Rooms are of cottage proportions; a small lounge with comfy chairs gathered round a blazing log fire, a cozy dining room where each small oak table is set with blue napkins, candles, willow-pattern china, and a tiny flower arrangement, and nine small, very plainly decorated bedrooms. Most visitors are attracted here for the outstanding dinners prepared by Eleanor. Dinner consists of an appetizer followed by a tasty homemade soup served with soda bread (the latter a popular fixture on the menu), a main course (with a vegetarian alternative), desserts, and cheese and biscuits. One-night or bed and breakfast only bookings are not usually accepted. The Lake District is a beautiful region, popular with walkers and sightseers alike. Some of its premier villages are Coniston, Hawkshead, Sawrey (home of Beatrix Potter), Ambleside, and Grasmere. *Directions:* Leave the M6 at junction 40 and take the A66 towards Keswick for 10 miles. The Mill is 2 miles north of this road and the signpost for Mungrisdale is midway between Penrith and Keswick.

THE MILL HOTEL
Owners Richard & Eleanor Quinlan
Mungrisdale
Penrith, Cumbria CA11 0XR
Tel: (07687) 79659
9 rooms, 7 with private bathrooms
From £30 per person dinner, B&B
Open February to October
Children welcome

This long, low, black and white timbered house, with portions dating from 1540, is home to Raewyn and Anthony Hackett-Jones and their three children. The main house is cottage-cozy and crammed with groupings of antique furniture and displays of Raewyn's collections of old-fashioned teapots and the like. Guests eat together around the dining room table and Raewyn cooks a three-course dinner with lots of choices to cater for various tastes. Many of the vegetables and fruits are grown in the garden. Three cozy, beamed bedrooms are in the main house, and four sunny rooms and a sitting room occupy a nearby converted stable block. The stable bedrooms are decorated with wall stenciling and patchwork quilts and each has a modern, color-coordinated bathroom. All is done with great style and a cozy, country informality prevails. A tennis court and above-ground swimming pool are available for guests' use. Breakfast is a treat with a variety of choices. One-night bookings are not accepted for weekends and guests are expected to dine here except on Sundays when they are directed to restaurants in the town. *Directions:* Take the A45 from Ipswich for 7 miles and exit for Needham Market (also signposted for the A140 Norwich). The private lane to Pipps Ford is an exit from the roundabout at the end of the slip road.

PIPPS FORD
Owners Raewyn & Anthony Hackett-Jones
Norwich Roundabout
Needham Market, Suffolk IP6 8LJ
Tel: (044979) 208
7 rooms with private bathrooms
From £22 per person
Closed Christmas
Credit cards MC, VS
Children welcome

The quiet, narrow country lane that runs in front of Fosse Farmhouse is the historical Fosse Way, the road built by the Romans to connect their most important forts from Devon to Lincolnshire. Caron Cooper has furnished her rooms with great flair using soft colors and enviable country-French antiques in every room. Charming collectibles and country china adorn much of the sitting and breakfast rooms and most pieces are for sale. Upstairs there are three extremely comfortable guest bedrooms. My favorite was The Pine Room with its mellow pine furniture and especially spacious, luxuriously equipped bathroom. Across the courtyard, the ground floor of the stables has been converted to a tearoom and restaurant. On the floor above, three cottage-style bedrooms are stylishly decorated in white on white. With advance notice Caron enjoys preparing an imaginative, three-course dinner, and is happy to cater to vegetarian palates. At Christmas time Caron offers a three-day festive holiday. This tranquil countryside setting is within an easy half hour's drive of Bath, Bristol, Tetbury, and Cirencester and the picture-perfect village of Castle Combe is also nearby. *Directions:* Exit the M4 at junction 17 towards Chippenham, turn right on the A420 (Bristol road) for 3 miles to the B4039 which you take around Castle Combe to The Gib where you turn left opposite The Salutation Inn. Fosse Farmhouse is on your right after 1 mile.

FOSSE FARMHOUSE
Owner Caron Cooper
Nettleton Shrub, Nettleton
Chippenham, Wiltshire SN14 7NJ
Tel: (0249) 782286
6 rooms with private bathrooms
From £30 per person
Open all year
Credit cards VS
Children welcome

Set in the picturesque moorland village of North Bovey, frequent winner of the best-kept Dartmoor village award, Gate House has a lovely location just behind the tree-lined village green. The location and warm welcome offered by hosts Margaret and John Tucker all add up to the perfect recipe for a countryside holiday. The sitting room has an ancient bread oven tucked inside a large stone fireplace beneath a low-beamed ceiling, and the dining room has a pine table in front of an atmospheric old stove. A narrow stairway leads up from the dining room to two of the guest bedrooms, each with a neat bathroom tucked under the eaves. The third bedroom is found at the top of another little staircase, this one off the Tuckers' sitting room, and affords views through a huge copper beech to the swimming pool and the countryside. Margaret loves to cook, but, on evenings when she does not, guests often eat at the adjacent Ring of Bells or at a traditional pub in one of the nearby villages. Apart from walking on the moor and touring the moorland villages, many guests enjoy golf at the nearby Manor Hotel. The Devon coastline is easily accessible and many guests enjoy a day trip into Cornwall, often venturing as far afield as Clovelly. *Directions:* From Exeter take the A38 to the A382, Bovey Tracy turnoff. Turn left in Mortenhampstead onto the Princetown road, then immediately left again to North Bovey, down the narrow lane into the village and Gate House is on the right three houses below the Ring of Bells.

GATE HOUSE
Owners Margaret & John Tucker
North Bovey, Devon TQ13 8RB
Tel: (0647) 40479
3 rooms with private bathrooms
From £20 per person
Closed Christmas & February
Children over 15
Wolsey Lodge

The Grange, a former rectory, is a rambling Regency home covered with wisteria, comfortably furnished by Sue and Malcolm Whittley. Guests are welcome to use the formal drawing room overlooking the vast expanses of sweeping lawn and mature trees, though most prefer the snug confines of the cozy television room. The four bedrooms range in size from a large twin room softly carpeted in pink with light pink walls and cushioned windowseats, to a compact double room with sunny yellow walls prettily furnished in country pine. Homey touches such as hanging bouquets of dried flowers, pictures on the walls, and even a Paddington bear on a corner shelf add warmth. Amidst the 5 acres of lawns and gardens, tucked behind the kitchen garden and beyond the ducks and peacocks, is a walled swimming pool. Northwold is within easy reach of Norwich with its splendid castle museum and cathedral, the ancient university town of Cambridge, the medieval market town of King's Lynn, and the unspoilt, scenic North Norfolk coast. Nearby are the Royal Family's summer home, Sandringham House, the Caley Mill lavender farm, and the church in Heacham where John Rolfe married his Indian princess, Pocohontas. *Directions:* From King's Lynn take the A134, signposted Thetford, to Northwold. Turn left into the village, pass the church and the Old Rectory (on the left) and turn left in front of the row of cottages which brings you into The Grange's driveway.

THE GRANGE
Owners Sue & Malcolm Whittley
Northwold
Thetford, Norfolk IP26 5NF
Tel: (0366) 728240
4 rooms, 2 with private bathrooms
From £15 per person
Closed Christmas
Children over 5

Transatlantic visitors to England making their way north will find that there is no finer introduction to English hospitality than spending the night in the home of Captain John and Eileen Stewart, just a one-hour drive via the motorway from Heathrow. Perhaps meander down the broad expanse of lawn bordered by the gently flowing mill stream and the ancient parish church, or stroll into the delightful market town before dinner. John, an enthusiastic cook, is happy to prepare dinners ranging from light suppers to gourmet treats, during which conversation is guaranteed to be lively, filled with wit and anecdotes from John's wartime exploits. Guests are encouraged to make themselves very much at home in the public rooms; the drawing room filled with military memorabilia and furnished with antiques and the upstairs lounge with its broad river views. A large and airy old-fashioned bedroom is in the Georgian part of the house overlooking the garden, and has its bathroom across the hall. Two additional bedrooms have modern ensuite bathrooms, views across the river and their beds have feather comforters. Guests often use The Mill House as a base from which to visit Oxford and Cambridge, both about an hour's drive away. *Directions:* Leave the M1 at exit 14, taking the A509 to Olney. The Mill House is at the end of Church Street adjacent to the parish church, the spire of which is the most prominent landmark in the town.

THE MILL HOUSE
Owners John & Eileen Stewart
Church Street
Olney, Buckinghamshire MK46 4AD
Tel: (0234) 711381
3 rooms with private bathrooms
From £23 per person
Closed Christmas
Children over 14
Wolsey Lodge

Otley House is an elegant home with soft carpets covering the gleaming wooden floors and lovely antiques gracing every room. This welcoming bed and breakfast is home to Michael and Lise Hilton and their children. Lise's Danish upbringing lends Scandinavian flair to the decor and cuisine of Otley House where the standards surpass those of many grand country house hotels. Up the grand Queen Anne staircase are four spacious bedrooms: Burgundy, Peach and Blue, are named for their color schemes, while Pine is named after its mellow old pine furniture. A ground-floor suite offers complete privacy with its separate entrance, sitting room, bedroom, and bathroom. Lise loves to entertain and is a stickler for using the freshest and best ingredients, in her cooking. She is helped in the house by two Danish students taking a year's break between school and university. After dinner, guests often enjoy a game of billiards in the billiard room. The superb comforts of the house and exquisite food merit a stay of several days. Unspoilt Suffolk villages are close at hand, Constable country is within easy reach as is Dunwich, the medieval village that has almost been claimed by the sea, the elegant seaside resort of Southwold, Minsmere Bird Reserve, and the concert hall at Snape. *Directions:* From Ipswich take the A12 (signposted Lowestoft) to Woodbridge, then turn left on the B1079 to Otley. Otley House is on the right after the post office.

OTLEY HOUSE
Owners Lise & Michael Hilton
Otley
Ipswich, Suffolk IP6 9NR
Tel: (0473) 890253
5 rooms with private bathrooms
From £40 double
Open March to November
Children over 12
Wolsey Lodge

The curious name of this house, recorded since 1690, is believed to be the locals' interpretation of *Bellus Mons,* for the beautiful mountain on which this cluster of fishing cottages stands. Hostess Bar Buchanan-Barber offers an especially warm welcome to guests along with tea and cakes in either the whitewashed courtyard, its walls hung with brimming baskets of flowers, or the tiny sitting room where a large old-fashioned chintz sofa and chairs are cozily drawn around the fire. The bedrooms are spacious, have low, curved ceilings, little windows set in thick walls, and share the facilities of an enormous bathroom. Bar enjoys sharing her love of Cornwall and the Cornish people, and thoroughly spoils her visitors. Penryn is a maze of streets and alleyways climbing up from the harbor, filled with a rugged charm, yet with none of the crowds and cuteness that plague the more well-known Cornish villages. Cornwall has an abundance of secluded river estuaries (the Helford estuary was Daphne du Maurier's setting for *Frenchman's Creek*), an abundance of gardens (Trelissick, Glendurgan, Trebah), and friendly villages down switchback lanes. *Directions:* From Truro take the A39 towards Falmouth. Ignore the first signpost into Penryn. At the traffic lights by the quay turn right up through the town. After the road forks and becomes one-way, slow down as Shute Lane is a narrow entrance between the houses on the right.

BELLA'S MOUSE
Owner Bar Buchanan-Barber
8 Shute Lane
Penryn, Cornwall TR10 8EY
Tel: (0326) 73433
2 rooms sharing 1 bathroom
From £16 per person
Closed Christmas
Children over 12
No Smoking house

The Gables is a quaint, thatched guesthouse near one of the most beautiful stretches of the Somerset coastline. Tucked away into a corner of the picturesque village of Porlock, this simple inn is most appealing on the outside, but within the decor of the rooms is very basic. An exception is the pretty dining room where guests eat breakfast in the morning looking out onto the especially pretty garden, filled in summertime with colorful flowers. All the guest rooms are spotlessly clean: those upstairs share two bathrooms while the twin-bedded one on the first floor has its own. If you want to stay in one of the quaint thatched cottages, so typical of this part of Somerset, and are looking for a warm welcome more than luxurious furnishings, then The Gables might make a good choice for accommodation. And it will certainly provide you with a convenient spot from which to explore this part of England. It is only a few minutes' drive down to the waterfront to Porlock's picturesque fishing port, or turn inland and the beauties of Exmoor unfold. This region where wild rivers plunge through wooded valleys and herds of wild ponies gallop free is where R. D. Blackmore set his famous novel *Lorna Doone*. *Directions:* Leave the M6 at junction 25 and take the A358 to the A39 Minehead road. Porlock is 6 miles west of Minehead on the A39. Overnight parking is found at the Information Centre car park, a short walk from The Gables.

THE GABLES
Owners Des & Betty Crick
Porlock
Somerset TA24 8LQ
Tel: (0643) 862552
7 rooms, 1 with private bathroom
From £16.50 per person
Closed Christmas
Children over 5

Shearings is an adorable, 16th-century thatched cottage sitting beside a winter stream in one of the prettiest villages in Hampshire, right on the edge of the New Forest. Positively bursting with old-world charm, the interior of Shearings has blackened oak beams, large inglenook fireplaces, and sloping floors. In fact, one of the most charming prospects of a stay here is the fact that there is not a straight wall or even floor in the house. For the duration of their stay Colin, a retired army brigadier, and his wife Rosemary "adopt" guests as family, sharing pre-dinner drinks, dinner, coffee, and conversation in front of the fire. A cocktail, wine, and coffee are included in the cost of the three-course dinner. Rosemary aims to provide good English cooking and guests can expect traditional choices such as roast lamb and lemon meringue pie. The bedrooms are very pretty; one has a bathroom ensuite and a single and double room share a bathroom. A small sitting room is packed with information to help guests plan their visits to the surrounding area. Salisbury is a short drive away and Stonehenge and the New Forest within easy reach. *Directions:* From Salisbury take the A354 towards Dorchester and after Combe Bissett (5 miles) turn left for Rockbourne. Shearings is on the left in the village, reached by a little bridge that spans the stream.

SHEARINGS
Owners Colin & Rosemary Watts
Rockbourne
Fordingbridge, Hampshire SP6 3NA
Tel: (07253) 256
3 rooms, 1 with private bathroom
From £20 per person
Open February to November
Children over 12

Few English guesthouses offer the ambience, warmth, and welcome of Mizzards Farm, a lovely, 16th-century farmhouse built of stone and brick. The setting is peaceful; the River Rother flowing through the 13 acres of gardens and fields, and the driveway winding through the large meadow-like front lawn past a small pond. The heart of the house, where breakfast is served, is especially inviting, with one wall filled by a massive inglenook fireplace and a staircase leading up to an open minstrels' gallery. In a newer wing, a sophisticated lounge is nicely furnished with antiques and highlighted by a grand piano. Twice a year concerts are held here. Mizzards Farm offers great comfort for the guest and each room has its own bathroom and color TV. The home was previously owned by an English rock star who converted the largest bedroom into a glitzy but fun theatrical showplace with a fancy bathroom featuring a marble bathtub. The other two guest rooms are smaller and are pleasantly decorated in more traditional decor. Dinner is not served, but there are many excellent choices of places to eat nearby. For the athletically minded, Mizzards also has a covered swimming pool for guests' use. *Directions:* From Petersfield take the A272 towards Midhurst. Turn right at the crossroads in Rogate, follow the road for 1 mile, cross the narrow bridge over the river and take the first right on the small lane up to Mizzards Farm.

MIZZARDS FARM
Owners J. & C. Francis
Rogate
Petersfield, Hampshire GU31 5HS
Tel: (0730) 821656
3 rooms with private bathrooms
From £36 double
Closed Christmas
Children over 6
No Smoking house

With a backdrop of mountain peaks and a lush green lawn sweeping down towards Rosthwaite village, The Hazel Bank Hotel has a superb location in Borrowdale, one of the loveliest and quietest Lake District valleys. The owners, Gwen and John Nuttall, assisted by family members Tony and Joan Doherty, have renovated this large Victorian residence, adding modern conveniences such as sparkling bathrooms to the bedrooms, all while keeping the house's period charm and character. All the rooms are light, airy, and uncluttered. The bedrooms are named after nearby mountains. The largest rooms are Scafell Pike, a twin-bedded room that overlooks the beginning of the Scafell range, and Great Gable where a four-poster bed and two substantial armchairs overlook the mountains through large windows. Dinner is served at 7:00 pm and a house party atmosphere prevails. John does most of the cooking and a measure of his success is the great number of returning guests, so bookings for one night or bed and breakfast only are not usually accepted. This is walking country so the hotel has a drying room for clothing and is happy to provide packed lunches. *Directions:* The hotel is located 7 miles south of Keswick on the B5289. Turn left over the little humped-back bridge just before entering Rosthwaite village.

THE HAZEL BANK HOTEL
Owners Gwen & John Nuttall
Rosthwaite
Borrowdale nr Keswick, Cumbria CA12 5XB
Tel: (07687) 77248
9 rooms with private bathrooms
From £30 per person dinner, B&B
Open mid-March to November
Children over 6

This solid stone cottage in the tiny village of Rowland is home to Mary Everard and her sleek black labrador Meg. Mary returned to her native Derbyshire after living in the United States for several years and converted her holiday home into an adorable little bed and breakfast. The large hall, paneled in golden oak with its matching staircase leading to the bedrooms, was once the living room of a much smaller cottage. Warmed in winter by a blazing log fire, the hall opens up to a country-style dining room with an old pine table and a softly carpeted sitting room with an array of brass fire equipment on the hearth. At the top of the stairs two prettily decorated twin bedrooms with views across the garden share one large bathroom. Mary asks guest to select their breakfast the night before so she can have it hot and ready, right on time. Bread is always homemade and yogurt and stewed fruit are available as well as the more usual cooked fare. The nearby Peak District National Park is a walker's paradise and the surrounding Derbyshire countryside offers picturesque walled fields and sturdy stone villages, highlighted in the summer when the villagers decorate their wells with floral designs. Also in the vicinity are Bakewell with its antique and tea shops and Monday market, Chatsworth House, and medieval Haddon Hall. *Directions:* Leave Bakewell over the bridge and follow the Hathersage road to Hassop. At Hassop, turn left up the hill for Rowland. After half a mile turn right and Holly Cottage is on the right.

HOLLY COTTAGE
Owner Mary Everard
Rowland
Bakewell, Derbyshire DE4 1NR
Tel: (062987) 624
2 rooms sharing 1 bathroom
From £14 per person
Closed November & December
Children welcome

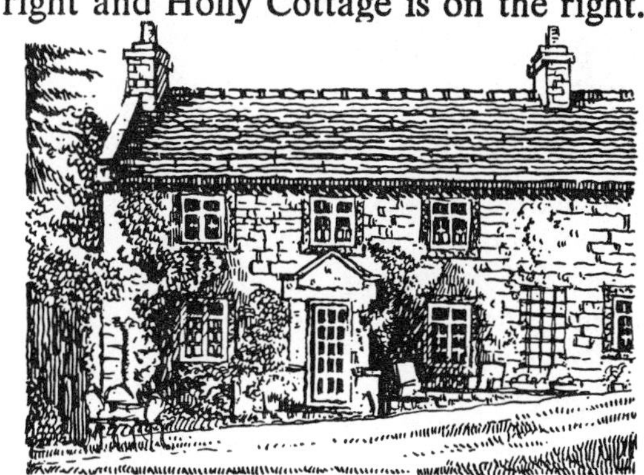

Local folklore is rich with tales of the smugglers and pirates who once frequented the many inlets of the St Just Peninsula in this unspoilt part of Cornwall. This scenic peninsula is now home to Treworga Farmhouse, where Brian and Kay Giffin offer homey accommodation to guests, encouraging them to make themselves at home and stop for a chat when entering the house. The guest bedroom is in fact a suite, having a large sitting room that could accommodate a third person, bedroom, and shower-room. Explorations of the peninsula yield quaint villages accessed by winding lanes. St Just in Roseland has an interesting churchyard full of sub-tropical plants planted by a vicar in the mid-1800s. St Mawes is a prosperous resort, its harbor filled with bobbing boats, and to the east, the villages of Portscatho, Veryan with its thatched circular houses, Portloe, and Mevagissey attract artists, writers, and throngs of tourists. King Harry Ferry takes travellers to Trelissick Gardens and south to Falmouth, the Lizard Peninsula, St Michaels Mount, and Lands End. *Directions:* From St Austell take the A390 following signs for St Mawes through Hewas Water and Tregony to Ruan High Lanes. Turn right at the Spar Grocers and gas pump, towards King Harry Ferry. Take the first right to the hamlet of Treworga and look for Treworga Farmhouse on the left.

TREWORGA FARMHOUSE
Owners Kay & Brian Giffin
Treworga
Ruan High Lanes
Truro, Cornwall TR2 5NP
Tel: (0872) 501423
1 bedroom with private bathroom
From £16 per person
Closed Christmas
Children over 5
No Smoking house

Rye, a busy port in medieval times, has become marooned 2 miles inland since the sea receded. Once the haunt of smugglers who climbed the narrow cobbled streets laden with booty from France, Rye is now a picturesque village which invites tourists to walk its cobbled lanes. The Jeake's House bed and breakfast dates back to 1690 when it was built by Samuel Jeake as a wool storehouse (wool was smuggled to France while brandy, lace, and salt were brought into England). Guests enter a tiny hallway-reception area from a doorway that opens directly onto the street. There is an intimate lounge area with a rather formal Victorian ambience. At some point in its history, the house was owned by the Baptist Church who built the chapel that is now the dining room of the inn, a surprisingly large, galleried hall where a roaring fire warms the room in winter. The guest rooms are attractively decorated in keeping with the historical mood of the house, each unique and furnished with antiques. All offer modern amenities such as tea making trays, television, and telephone and all but two have a private bathroom. Within easy driving distance are Winchelsea, Battle Abbey (built on the site of the Battle of Hastings in 1066), Bodiam Castle, and Sissinghurst Gardens. *Directions:* Rye is between Folkestone and Hastings on the A259. Mermaid Street is the main street in town, and Jeake's House is near the Mermaid Inn.

JEAKE'S HOUSE
Owners Francis & Jenny Hadfield
Mermaid Street
Rye, Sussex TN31 7ET
Tel: (0797) 222828 fax: (0797) 225758
12 rooms, 10 with private bathrooms
From £19 per person
Open all year
Credit cards MC, VS
Children welcome

Rye is one of England's most enchanting towns and Little Orchard House is one of Rye's most engaging small bed and breakfasts. The location is ideal, right in the heart of town on a small lane leading off Mermaid Street. Don't miss the inn's discreet sign. An archway captures a most inviting little courtyard faced by a pretty, peaches-and-cream-colored house with a happy bright red door. Inside there is no formal reception area: registration takes place in the cozy, country-style kitchen which opens onto a very large garden. Guests are welcome to stroll through the old-fashioned walled garden where paths meander through colorful beds of flowers. In one corner of the garden a red brick tower rises, once used by smugglers to signal if the coast was clear. The guest rooms are reached by a staircase leading up from the cozy study with its large open fireplace. Each of the bedrooms is different in decor yet each maintains a cheerful mood. Nothing is contrived or cutesy; all is very inviting. The very friendly owners, Robert and Geraldine Bromley, are highly involved in the management of their bed and breakfast and personally see that each guest is made welcome and pampered. *Directions:* Follow signs to the town center and enter via the old Landgate Arch. West Street is the third street on the left off the High Street.

LITTLE ORCHARD HOUSE
Owners Geraldine & Robert Bromley
West Street
Rye, Sussex TN31 7ES
Tel: (0797) 223831
3 rooms with private bathrooms
From £35 per person
Open all year
Credit cards MC, VS
No children
Wolsey Lodge

Atop the quaint cobbled streets of Rye is the ancient church and churchyard of St Mary's, surrounded by a square of delightful old houses. Fortunately for visitors to this picturesque town, one of these, The Old Vicarage (a dusty pink Georgian house with white trim and twin chimneys), is run as a guesthouse by a delightful young couple, Julia and Paul Masters. Since they bought the inn a few years ago, they have been constantly upgrading and refurbishing the rooms. All of the guest rooms are decorated with Laura Ashley fabrics: two have four-poster beds and one has a coronet-style draped headboard. Each of the guest rooms has color TV, hairdryer, and tea tray. There are also some small, but cozy, less expensive rooms tucked under the eaves on the top floor--these three bedrooms share a bathroom. The Garden Suite, a large family room with a sitting area, is below stairs. The ambience throughout the inn is one of homey comfort. On summer weekends, Julia and Paul offer a traditional afternoon tea in the garden. Overnight car parking is provided across the square in a residents-only parking area. If you write ahead, the Masters will send you a brochure with a map on just how to find them amongst the maze of Rye's narrow cobblestoned streets. Rye deserves a visit of several days to explore its narrow cobbled streets, antique and craft shops and old fortifications. *Directions:* Rye is on the A259 between Folkestone and Hastings.

THE OLD VICARAGE GUEST HOUSE
Owners Julia & Paul Masters
66 Church Square
Rye, Sussex TN31 7HF
Tel: (0797) 222119
6 rooms, 3 with private shower
From £19 per person
2-night weekend minimum stay during season
Closed Christmas
Children over 12

Perched high on a steep, wooded cliff, Courtenay House occupies one of the most spectacular sites in this book. The view looks straight out over the trees to a golden beach in the small cove of South Sands, to the blue waters of the Salcombe estuary and to the sea beyond, dotted with sailboats. Courtenay House was built to maximize these vistas; a terrace opens up from the sitting/dining room (breakfast is served here on fine summer mornings) and a balcony runs the length of three of the bedrooms. The house is decorated to give a feel of airy spaciousness, and all four bedrooms have spectacular views. Guests share two large bathrooms and an additional WC across the hall. Terracing down to the Salcombe estuary, Salcombe is Devon's loveliest seaside resort, and sailing is a popular pastime. Other attractions include Sharpitor, the coastal heritage walk, and the spectacular coastal scenery from Bolt Head. Nearby lie the old market town of Kingsbridge and Dartmouth with its picturesque quays and quaint buildings. *Directions:* From the A38 take the A384 towards Totnes to the A381 Kingsbridge road. Follow signs for Salcombe around Kingsbridge. After passing the Salcombe Mayflower garage on the right, take the second right (Sandhills Road), another right at the T-junction, pass the beach, and take a sharp left up the hill. Fork right at the top and Courtenay House is the first house on the left.

COURTENAY HOUSE
Owners Tricia & Tim Tucker
Moult Hill
Salcombe, Devon TQ8 8LF
Tel: (054884) 2761
4 rooms sharing 2 1/2 bathrooms
From £21.50 per person
Closed Christmas
Children over 8
Wolsey Lodge

Stratford Lodge is tucked down a quiet lane overlooking a large park just a few minutes' drive from the center of Salisbury. Jill Bayly runs the house as a home rather than a traditional guesthouse, so guests have the use of a large sitting room and the adjacent entrance hall is lined with books galore, many of them useful in planning sightseeing adventures. Pretty wallpapers and fabrics, pastel color schemes, antiques, flowers, and family mementos combine to give the bedrooms a home-like charm and all have a tea tray and biscuits, TV, and private bathroom. At the time of our visit the finishing touches were just being completed on a new wing--these guest rooms will be especially nice, so request one when making a reservation. Jill is an excellent cook and provides a delicious set meal with advance reservations: a typical dinner might consist of baked pears with Roquefort, roast duckling in a black cherry and port sauce, apple strudel with clotted cream, and cheese. Fruit from the garden is usually offered for breakfast and, instead of bacon and eggs, guests may try mushrooms on toast or smoked haddock kedgeree. In addition to Salisbury's old streets and cathedral, Stonehenge and Avebury's megalithic monuments are close at hand while Bath, the New Forest, Winchester, and Southampton are easy day trips. *Directions:* As you enter Salisbury on the A345, from Amesbury, take the first right-hand turn (at the shop) onto Park Lane.

STRATFORD LODGE
Owner Jill Bayly
4 Park Lane, off Castle Road
Salisbury, Wiltshire SP1 3NP
Tel: (0722) 25177
8 rooms with private bathrooms
From £25 per person
Closed Christmas
Children over 5
No Smoking house

In her younger years Beatrix Potter used to visit Ees Wyke House with her family. Over the ensuing years the house has been transformed into the pleasant, traditional guesthouse today run by John and Mag Williams who have painted and decorated the house from top to bottom in a comfortable style that they enjoy. John, a former cookery teacher at a catering college, offers very nicely prepared, traditional English dinners with choices for all of the courses. The Williams have a good sense of humor and enjoy meeting guests from all different walks of life, offering an unpretentious north-country welcome. The bedrooms have lovely countryside views and many overlook nearby Esthwaite Water. The two attic bedrooms were added in 1990; one has a bathroom ensuite while the other has a private bath just next door. The other bedrooms also have a mix of ensuite and adjacent bathroom arrangements. The smallest bedroom, on the ground floor, is reserved for visitors who have difficulty with stairs, and unfortunately has no view. A short walk into the village leads to Hill Top Farm where Beatrix Potter wrote several of her books. Walks abound in the area and the more oft trod Lakeland routes are easily accessible by taking the nearby ferry across Lake Windermere. *Directions:* From Ambleside take the A593 towards Coniston. After about a mile turn left on the B5286 to Hawkshead. Skirt Hawkshead village and follow signs for the ferry. Ees Wyke House is on the right just before you come into Sawrey.

EES WYKE COUNTRY GUEST HOUSE
Owners John & Mag Williams
Near Sawrey
Ambleside, Cumbria LA22 0JZ
Tel: (09666) 393
8 rooms with private bathrooms
From £24 per person
Closed January
Children over 10 & babies

This Suffolk farmhouse stands amidst fields and woods in a quiet country location where for over 400 years it was a working farm. Hostess Mary's caring ways are evident in the quiet, warm way she treats her guests. Her welcome is seconded by handsome George, a tail-wagging dog, and Lizzie, a collie who loves to "mother" youngsters. Families with children are welcome here, though parents must supervise young ones on the narrow spiral staircase. Mary's old paintings, antique furniture, and books galore fit happily into this mellow, beamed house. Pink-toned armchairs and a long sofa border an oriental carpet in front of the wood-burning stove in the living room. The food served in the book-lined dining room is excellent: a typical meal might be asparagus and salmon mousse, lamb chops with fresh vegetables and new potatoes, and a choice of desserts. The large principal bedroom has a bathroom ensuite while three smaller bedrooms share a bathroom and an additional WC (with a maximum of six guests at a time the facilities are never overtaxed). Nearby are Blythburgh with its 15th-century church, Dunwich, the medieval village almost claimed by the sea, Southwold, Minsmere Bird Reserve, and the concert hall at Snape. *Directions:* From Ipswich take the A12 (signposted Lowestoft). Between Yoxford and Blythburgh take the lane beside "The Happy Eater" (on the right) and look for High Poplars on the right after 1 1/2 miles.

HIGH POPLARS
Owner Mary Montague
Hinton
Saxmundham, Suffolk IP17 3RJ
Tel: (050270) 528
4 rooms, 1 with private bathroom
From £18 per person
Open all year
Children welcome
Wolsey Lodge

Overlooking the spacious village green opposite Saxtead's windmill, The Limes Farmhouse is a bed and breakfast where guests are encouraged to make themselves at home in a very casual atmosphere. Guest rooms occupy an upstairs wing of the house and consist of an especially nice large twin room with ensuite bathroom and two very small double rooms whose bathroom is down the hall. In summer the garden is a riot of heavily scented color, but parents must keep young children close at hand as beyond the flowerbeds lies an unprotected moat and beyond the garden is a duckpond. Tiny Shetland ponies trot to the fence in the hope that visitors will have brought a treat. Warm summer mornings find guests seated on the terrace for breakfast; alternatively, they can pamper themselves with a breakfast tray in their room. Saxtead's windmill is open to the public every day except Sunday. The most popular places to visit are Framlingham and Orford Castle, Woodbridge, and Easton Farm Park. Garden lovers will enjoy Notcutts, Helmingham, and Charlesfield, while the coastal villages of Southwold, Walberswick, and Dunwich are close at hand. Constable country and Snape Maltings, home of the Benjamin Britten music festival, are also very popular. *Directions:* From Ipswich take the A12 (Lowestoft) to Wickham Market then turn left on the B1116 through Framlingham to Saxtead Green. The Limes Farmhouse is the black and white farmhouse across the green from the windmill.

THE LIMES FARMHOUSE
Owners Carole & Michael Albrecht
Saxtead Green
Framlingham, Suffolk IP13 9QH
Tel: (0728) 82303, fax: (0728) 82825
3 rooms, 1 with private bathroom
From £20 per person
Closed Christmas
Children welcome

Longdon Manor is an absolutely delightful home tucked deep in the countryside, fronted by rambling outbuildings and picturesque barns and backed by a grassy garden whose centerpiece is a tall, 17th-century dovecote. The sitting room invites guests to stretch out in a chair before the log fire, gently play the concert grand, or browse through piles of sheet music and books. The polished flagstones, high ceilings, and deeply set mullioned windows echo days long past, for this was a residence hall as early as the 14th century, with additions being made in the 16th and 17th centuries. The dining room walls are hung with family photos, a deep window niche displays fossils and seashells, and the elegant table is laid with country-style crockery. With advance notice Jane is happy to provide dinner. The bedrooms are all different; a cottage-style twin nestles under the eaves, a large double has lavishly painted and gilded French furniture, and another exquisitely furnished double has a flamboyant bathroom. Although Jane does not usually take reservations on weekends, she often accepts guests who would like to attend one of the informal concerts held here once a month. Longdon Manor is perfect for exploring the Cotswold villages and visiting the theater at Stratford-on-Avon. *Directions:* From Shipston-on-Stour take the B4035 towards Chipping Campden. Cross the A429 and after half a mile turn right towards Darlingscott. After a mile the lane bends sharp right while the drive to Longdon Manor is straight ahead.

LONGDON MANOR
Owners Jane Brabyn & family
Shipston-on-Stour, Warwickshire CV36 4PW
Tel: (060882) 235
3 rooms with private bathrooms
From £30 per person
Open all year - Monday to Thursday
Children welcome
Wolsey Lodge

Speen Cottage is less than two hours' drive from Heathrow airport, most of it via motorway, making this a well-placed starting or finishing point for visitors to the west of England. After a refreshing cup of tea guests can relax in the garden, swim in the pool, or take a stroll before dinner. The traditional, bay-windowed sitting room with its soft cream carpet topped with an oriental rug is light, airy, and spacious and Pamela's stitchery decorates cushions, banners, bellpulls, footstools, and chaircovers. The dining room is furnished with rugged light oak furniture from "mouse man" Robert Thompson of Yorkshire, whose small church mouse signature is on each piece. The two twin-bedded rooms have their private bathrooms across the hall, and there is also an additional small single room which, if occupied, shares one of the same baths. In the vicinity are a number of very attractive Berkshire villages and the Vale of the White Horse. A number of historic towns are within an hour's drive: Oxford, Bath, Windsor, Salisbury, Hungerford, and Marlborough. *Directions:* Leave the M4 at exit 13 and take the A4 to Newbury. Drive through the town (towards Hungerford), climb the hill, curve left after the Hare and Hounds then turn immediately left into Speen Lane. In 200 yards enter the large white gates of Speen Cottage on the left.

SPEEN COTTAGE
Owner Pamela Walsh
Speen Lane, Speen
Newbury, Berkshire RG13 1RJ
Tel: (0635) 40859
3 rooms, 2 with private bathrooms
From £20 per person
Open all year
No children
No Smoking house
Wolsey Lodge

Downhayes is a traditional, 16th-century country farmhouse located in the lovely rolling hills of Devon. The very simplicity of this two-story, white-washed home adds to its charm. The day we arrived, Tom was puttering in the front garden while Prue, apron around her waist, appeared from the large kitchen from which wafted the aroma of freshly baked cake. Inside, Downhayes' decor is lovely. Not stuffy or elaborate, just with a simple, inviting ambience, perfectly reflecting the country feel of the home. Prue, with advance notice, serves dinner for her guests in a cozy dining room overlooking the back garden. I highly recommend visitors dining here as the food is excellent, served by candlelight with fine china, crystal, and silverware. Before the meal, guests gather in front of the open hearth in the beamed sitting room. A ground floor guest room has windows opening onto the garden, but my favorite room is the corner bedroom upstairs furnished with light wood antique furniture. A third, very pretty bedroom has its bathroom down the hall. Downhayes is close to Dartmoor made famous by Sir Arthur Conan Doyle in *The Hounds of the Baskervilles*. The north and south Devon coasts are within easy reach and fishing and golf are available nearby. *Directions:* Leave the M5 at exit 31 and take the A30 towards Okehampton, leaving it at Whiddon Down and following signs for Spreyton. Downhayes is on the left between Spreyton and Bow.

DOWNHAYES
Owners Prue and Tom Hines
Spreyton
Crediton, Devon EX17 5AR
Tel: (03633) 378
3 rooms with private bathrooms
From £20 per person
Closed Christmas
Children over 12
Wolsey Lodge

This lovely Georgian home set in 5 acres of grounds in peaceful countryside offers outstanding accommodations. Rashleigh is an enormous room and its double bed has an artfully draped bedhead matching the curtains and bedspread. Treffry, a twin-bedded room in delicate shades of lemon, has decorative flowers stenciled on the wall behind the beds, and Prideaux has a dainty, white four-poster bed draped with a pink and white flowery fabric. Each bedroom has an elegant ensuite bathroom with spa bath, down comforters, tea and coffee makings, television, and direct dial telephone. Guests have their own entrance into a lofty hallway whose table is used for dining (with advanced notice). Double doors open up to a vast sitting room which is for guests' exclusive use. Outside you find a swimming pool and paved terrace with views across rolling countryside. Local attractions include the picturesque town of Fowey, the fishing village of Mevagissey, the cathedral city of Truro, Bodmin Moor, and many unusual exhibitions and museums. Daphne Du Maurier's novel *All the King's Men* is set around St Blazey. *Directions:* Pass over the Tamar Bridge into Cornwall and follow signs to Liskeard. Take the A390 (St Austell turnoff) following it through Lostwithiel and into St Blazey. Cross the railway lines and opposite the Texaco garage turn right into Prideaux road following it up the hill until you see Nanscawen on your right.

NANSCAWEN
Owners Janet & Keith Martin
Prideaux Road, St Blazey
Par, Cornwall PL24 2SR
Tel: (072681) 4488
3 rooms with private bathrooms
From £22.50 per person
Closed Christmas
Children over 12
No Smoking house

Breathtaking, panoramic views of the Wye Valley open up from Cinderhill House, a pink-washed cottage whose core dates back to the 14th century with additions over the years. Gillie is a warm and friendly hostess who enjoys welcoming guests to her lovely home. Bedrooms in the main house are very prettily decorated and all have tea and coffee trays. An additional attic room with twin beds and a crib is reserved for children so that parents can put their children to bed and go downstairs for dinner. Two plainer rooms are in the adjacent converted stables. Breakfast is a treat: fruit compotes and cold cereals are followed by hot dishes such as fresh salmon fishcakes and herb omelets, yet Gillie considers dinner her forte! On chilly evenings a crackling log fire invites guests into the large sitting room to enjoy a drink before dinner. On the night of my visit dinner was a salad of grapes, apples, and watermelon with a sour cream and mint dressing, honey roast duck and fresh vegetables, lemon meringue pie, cheeseboard, and coffee. Gillie's three-night Christmas and New Year's parties are something guests look forward to. Apart from enjoying the peace and quiet of the Wye Valley and the Forest of Dean, guests venture farther afield to Bristol, Cardiff, Gloucester, Cheltenham, Bath, and Hereford. *Directions:* Take the M4 from Bristol over the Severn Bridge to exit 22 for Monmouth. Follow the A466 for 7 miles, turn right over the Bigsweir bridge for St Briavels. Continue 1 1/2 miles up to St Briavels castle and Cinderhill House is on the left just before the castle.

CINDERHILL HOUSE
Owner Gillie Peacock
St Briavels, Gloucestershire GL15 6HR
Tel: (0594) 530393
5 rooms with private bathrooms
From £19 per person
Open all year
Children welcome

The Old Rectory was built in the 13th century as the home for priests of the nearby church so Pat and Bob Claridge have named their four rooms after former incumbents. The grandest room has an imposing four-poster bed and windows overlooking the garden and river, while a large double room has a brass and iron bed and beamed walls and ceiling with an adjacent twin-bedded room which is perfect for children, auntie, or mum. All bedrooms have fluffy bathrobes, tea and coffee trays, and color television. For relaxation guest can use the cozy downstairs reception room where large chairs are gathered before a log fire or the very elegant drawing room whose gray moire silk drapes artistically frame the large garden windows. Bob and Pat's standards of welcome match the comfort of this lovely home. It is a fast hour's drive via the motorway from Heathrow airport to Oxford and from there less than a half hour to Standlake, making this an ideal "jumping off point" for an English holiday for overseas visitors. Blenheim Palace and gardens, Oxford, and the White Horse are close by, and just a little farther afield lie the picturesque Cotswold villages. *Directions:* From Oxford take the A420 signposted Swindon for 6 miles and the A415 signposted Witney for 4 miles to Standlake. Turn right at the garage ("Village Only") and after a mile keep left at the small triangular green and The Old Rectory is on the right, opposite the school.

THE OLD RECTORY
Owners Pat & Bob Claridge
Standlake
Witney, Oxfordshire OX8 7SG
Tel: (0865) 300559
4 rooms with private bathrooms
Double from £36 to £66.50
Closed December & January
Children welcome

Hilltop has been in host Tim Rathmell's family since it was built in 1640; quite an impressive record! Tim and his wife, Marie-Louise, have tastefully modernized the house adding ensuite bathrooms while keeping and exposing lovely features such as the beef loft in the beamed dining room where beef used to be hung to dry above the open fire. They have made the old stables into their home and enjoy welcoming guests to the main house. Four bedrooms with light and airy decor contain spacious king-sized beds and have showers in the bathrooms. The fifth bedroom is a snug, flowery twin and enjoys a large bathroom with a claw-foot tub. Ancient family documents decorate the tiny bar where guests gather to chat over drinks. Tim puts his heart into his cooking and concentrates on properly cooked vegetables and sauces to accompany the main course while Marie-Louise is in charge of dessert which may be a specialty from her German homeland. After dinner guests enjoy the cheer of a blazing log fire in the sitting room or, on warm summer evenings, stretch their legs strolling in the foothills behind Hilltop or down to the village pub. Walks abound in this lovely part of the Yorkshire Dales, and car touring is just as enjoyable, offering castles, country homes, and the abbeys of North Yorkshire. A scenic 70-mile round-trip route from Hilltop includes Kilnsey Crag, Malham Tarn, Gordale Scar, and Stump Cross Caverns. *Directions:* Starbotton is in Wharfedale, 16 miles north of Skipton on the B6160.

HILLTOP COUNTRY GUEST HOUSE
Owners Marie-Louise & Tim Rathmell
Starbotton
Skipton, Yorkshire BD23 5HY
Tel: (075676) 321
5 rooms with private bathrooms
From £24 per person
Open mid-March to mid-November
Children welcome

Kingston House is one of the grandest houses in this book, a spectacular example of an early Georgian baroque home returned to its former glory. A crackling log fire blazes in the massive grate in the entrance hall which is also a spectacular setting for dining with Mike and Elizabeth on cool winter evenings. The main staircase, covered with inlaid wood, is an impressive piece of workmanship. The cozy study and elegant drawing room are found behind 8-foot-tall doors. The old family chapel is now a pleasant sitting room with a TV concealed in a corner cabinet and ancient wall paintings hidden behind peeling paint (Elizabeth's next restoration project). The bedrooms are elegant; Rowe's is decorated in 1740s style in gold and red with a large ensuite bathroom. Rendell's is in 1830s style and contains the original four-poster bed made for the room--its large bathroom is across the hall. The master suite's bedroom has a grand angel-tester bed with swathes of bright fabric matching the curtains, and dark sage green painted paneling, with a claw-foot tub in the bathroom. The scenic beauty of Devon is on the doorstep; beyond the narrow country lane to Staverton, "A" roads give easy access to Dartmoor and both Devon coasts. *Directions:* Leave the A38 at the A384 Totnes road and after 2 miles turn left to Staverton, bearing left at the railway station. After passing the Sea Trout Inn on the right take the next lane on the left to Kingston.

KINGSTON HOUSE
Owners Elizabeth & Mike Corfield
Staverton
Totnes, Devon TQ9 6AR
Tel: (080426) 235
3 rooms with private bathrooms
From £40 per person
Closed Christmas
Credit cards MC, VS
No children

Only the most detailed maps pinpoint Curdon Mill in the hamlet of Vellow, but your endeavors to find this lovely valley close to the sea and near the beautiful Quantock hills are rewarded. The approach to the mill skirts Daphne and Richard Criddle's farm. A few years ago they decided to renovate the old water mill on their property, adding a lounge where guests can relax and browse through books describing sights to see in the area. The mill shaft hangs across the ceiling in the dining room and the restaurant is open to the public for a set dinner menu. Residents can order in advance from an extensive a la carte menu that is sent to them when their booking is confirmed. Of the six bedrooms my favorite is the Stag Room which was named because deer can sometimes be seen in the fields below the window. The Criddles have also created a lovely flower garden and even nestled a small swimming pool on a terrace near the inn. Although the accommodations offer modern amenities, the surroundings are definitely rural as this is a working farm where you can enjoy watching the farm animals, taking walks, or even trout fishing. Exmoor National Park is nearby, a region of spectacular scenery that varies from rolling, green farmland to wild heathland. *Directions:* Leave the M25 at Taunton and take the A358 towards Williton. Curdon Mill is 2 1/2 miles southwest of Williton on the Stogumber road before the hamlet of Vellow.

CURDON MILL
Owners Daphne & Richard Criddle
Lower Vellow, Stogumber
Taunton, Somerset TA4 4LS
Tel: (0984) 56522
6 rooms with private bathrooms
From £20 per person
Open all year
Children over 10
No Smoking house

The food at The Angel Inn is outstanding and, fortunately for visitors to this pretty part of Suffolk, guests may lodge as well as dine here. When Peter Smith and Richard Wright purchased the inn in 1985 it was in a sorry state, but now its complete refurbishment has transformed it into a building with lots of charm and old-world ambience. Guests eating in the bar on a weekend are best advised to avoid the crush by arriving early (or just before last orders at 9:00 pm), make their selection from the menu hung on the old, red-brick wall above the fireplace and then settle down at one of the tables grouped under the low-beamed ceiling. Those preferring a more formal meal or quieter atmosphere may elect to dine in the restaurant where tables can be reserved in either of the two dining rooms. One is a cozy room with pine paneling, the other more dramatic, with ceilings removed to expose lofty rafters. Tables are laid with starched linen and soft lighting adds a romantic mood. The menu offers several choices of starters and main courses including a good selection of fresh seafood. Bedrooms are pleasantly furnished and have a light, airy decor. This unspoilt region of quiet countryside offers lots of sightseeing, such as the nearby valley of the River Stour, Dedham, and Flatford Mill, all made famous by John Constable's paintings. *Directions:* Take the A134 Sudbury road from Colchester for 5 miles to Nayland, then turn left for the 2-mile drive to Stoke by Nayland.

THE ANGEL INN
Owners Richard Wright & Peter Smith
Stoke by Nayland
Colchester, Essex CO6 4SA
Tel: (0206) 263245
6 rooms with private bathrooms
From £25 per person
Closed Christmas
Children over 12

Parts of Swalcliffe Manor date back to the 13th century and it is noted as being the oldest stone-built manor house in Oxfordshire. An unusual architectural feature of the home is the giant vaulted undercroft, a series of interconnecting stone arches and pillars, such as is usually found in the crypts of ancient churches. Its cold flagstone floor and sturdy arches open up to a hallway which leads to the great hall, a vast room that was modernized in 1480 when a giant fireplace was built and bedrooms were added above. It is here that guests warm their toes and enjoy a drink in front of the fire before going in to dinner. The dining room, by contrast with the great hall, is cozy and intimate. A typical dinner might include salmon mousse, poached chicken in tarragon sauce, strawberry pavlova, and a cheeseboard. A wide hallway leads to the bedrooms, one of which occupies what used to be the children's nurseries. The most attractive bedroom has a large four-poster bed and an arched stone doorway leading to the bathroom. Visitors often use Swalcliffe Manor as a base for visiting the Cotswolds, Oxford, Blenheim Palace, Stratford-on-Avon, and Warwick Castle. *Directions:* Swalcliffe is midway between Banbury and Shipston-on-Stour on the B4035. The entrance to the Manor is on the main road next to the church.

SWALCLIFFE MANOR
Owners Judith & Francis Hitching
Swalcliffe
Banbury, Oxfordshire OX15 5EH
Tel: (029578) 348
3 rooms with private bathrooms
From £19 to £28 per person
Open March to November
Children over 7
Wolsey Lodge

Imagine enjoying the sky-wide vistas of the Suffolk countryside from a horse and carriage which, after a delicious meal at an old-fashioned thatch-roofed pub, will convey you home to Tannington Hall and hosts Sheila and Tony Harvey. Their bed and breakfast is a large 16th-century moated farmhouse set deep in the countryside. This pleasantly old-fashioned house has two twin-bedded guest bedrooms and a single room that all share two bathrooms. Sheila is happy to provide a light supper or a full evening meal, her specialty being traditional English food, or, if a more gourmet meal is desired, daughter Judith, a Cordon Bleu chef, is pleased to oblige. Across the driveway, through the stables lies the carriage barn containing Tony's collection of horse-drawn vehicles from sturdy wagons to brightly painted gypsy caravans. An immaculate green lawn sweeps away to the garden where little paths wind between heavily scented roses to the moat. Beyond the garden lies the working part of the farm--a vast piggery full of pink pigs of all sizes. Close by is Framlingham Castle and its medieval church. Thirty minutes away lie Minsmere Bird Reserve, Aldeburgh, and Snape Maltings. *Directions:* From Ipswich take the A12, towards Lowestoft, to Wickham Market, then turn left on the B1116 through Framlingham to Saxtead Green. Cross the green and follow signs for Tannington. Tannington Hall is well signposted on the outskirts of the village.

TANNINGTON HALL
Owners Sheila & Tony Harvey
Tannington
Woodbridge, Suffolk IP13 7NH
Tel: (072876) 226
3 rooms sharing 2 bathrooms
From £20 per person
Closed Christmas
Children welcome
Wolsey Lodge

It is said that Admiral Lord Nelson and the Duke of Wellington were once guests at Littleburn and the conviviality of those long-ago house-parties is still echoed today in Diana and Donald Cameron's soirees. They have lived all over the world and have always enjoyed entertaining and welcoming visitors; the only difference nowadays is that guests are paying bed-and-breakfast patrons. Early arrivals are welcomed with tea, shown to their rooms and invited to join Donald and Diana for pre-dinner drinks in the drawing room which, paneled in old pine and overlooking green fields and hills across the lawn, is a particularly attractive room. In the dining room the elegant table is laid with Waterford crystal and silver service. After dinner, guests are settled in the drawing room to be joined for conversation and drinks by their hosts and the friendly King Charles spaniels Bunty and Poppy who affectionately vie for visitors' attentions. On chilly evenings an open log fire adds cheer to the occasion. There are many spots to visit including Aysgarth Falls, Malham Tarn, Hardraw Falls, Jervaulx Abbey, Fountains Abbey, and Newby Hall and gardens. *Directions:* Turn south to Thoralby from the A684 just east of Aysgarth village. Upon entering Thoralby, turn right at the post office/shop onto a minor road. Pass the George Inn on the right and bear left at the next fork for Littleburn; the house is on the right just after the little bridge.

LITTLEBURN
Owners Diana & Donald Cameron
Thoralby
Leyburn, Yorkshire DL8 3BE
Tel: (09693) 621
3 rooms with private bathrooms
From £24.50 per person
Closed christmas
No children
Wolsey Lodge

The quiet village of Thornton Rust is in the heart of the Yorkshire Dales and Thornton Rust Hall nestles below green rocky fields within a sheltered, flower-filled garden. The Hall, dating from 1667 and 1702, underwent a complete and careful restoration just before the Coopers moved in. (Gillian and Alan added an indoor heated swimming pool and a hard tennis court.) Upstairs, two large sunny bedrooms have their bathrooms ensuite while two additional bedrooms share a bathroom. Gillian ensures that guests are well looked after and well fed. Guests dine together round the dining room table and a typical main course might be a traditional roast beef accompanied by vegetables fresh from the garden. After dinner guests can enjoy a game of billiards in the enormous billiard room or retire to the cozy sitting room to enjoy homemade brandy snaps and coffee. With a lifetime spent in the Yorkshire Dales, Gillian and Alan are happy to assist in planning driving tours that encompass the stunning scenery and visit the market towns made famous by the Herriot television series. The ancient castles at Bolton, Skipton, and Middleham and the old abbeys of Jervaulx, Fountains, and Bolton are also worth a visit. The Hall also has three self-catering cottages available for weekly rentals. *Directions:* Leave the A1 at Leeming Bar and take the A684 via Bedale and Leyburn to Aysgarth where there is a left turn for Thornton Rust.

THORNTON RUST HALL
Owners Gillian & Alan Cooper
Thornton Rust
Leyburn, Yorkshire DL8 3AW
Tel: (0969) 663569
4 rooms, 2 with ensuite bathrooms
From £28 per person
Closed Christmas
Children over 8
Wolsey Lodge

Southover House is a picture-perfect, Jacobean-style manor house set in 6 acres of garden which stretch out to 100 acres of rolling hills. Although quite grand, there is a most welcoming ambience to this beautiful stone home whose many-gabled roof-line is accented by a profusion of high chimneys hinting of cozy fires within. Driving into the courtyard, my first impression was that this must be a fancy hotel, yet it is run as a bed and breakfast, offering guests a taste of the best of country living. An elaborate open staircase wraps around the hallway to the upper floor where two very spacious guest rooms, each with large private bathroom, are light and airy, with large windows opening onto the back garden. A third single bedroom is located across the hallway. Breakfast is served in the splendid paneled dining room. If the day is warm, guests enjoy the pool to the side of the house and Michael Slocock, a delightfully charming host, shows off the field behind the house where friends gather for enthusiastic cricket matches. Michael's brother, Richard, has a fly fishing school next door and many guests find fly fishing in the nearby lakes and rivers while living in elegant comfort at Southover House the perfect holiday combination. Southover is well placed for exploring Hardy Country and the Dorset coast. Tolpuddle gained instant fame in 1834 when six agricultural workers were shipped off to Australia for banding together to fight low wages. *Directions:* From Dorchester take the A35 northeast for 5 miles to Tolpuddle.

SOUTHOVER HOUSE
Owners Leslie & Michael Slocock
Tolpuddle
Dorchester, Dorset DT2 7HF
Tel: (0305) 848220 fax: (0305) 848516
3 rooms with private bathrooms
From £20 per person
Closed Christmas
Children welcome

Upton House, a 12th-century village manor house, offers guests a winning combination: a lovely house with country cottage coziness, outstanding decor, treasured antiques, carefully tended, flower-filled gardens, and a charming hostess. In the sitting room plump sofas covered in soft pink or blue brocade are grouped before the fireplace. In the adjacent dining room soft primrose walls highlight the blackened beams and a log fire blazes in the fireplace whose ornate pine mantle is decked with delicate china. From the dining room a private staircase leads to the Pink Bedroom, a twin-bedded room where everything from the tiny flowered bag containing guest soap to the pretty floral curtains coordinates with the muted pink walls. Up the main cottage staircase are the equally lovely Peach and Blue rooms. Angela has paid attention to the smallest details; tea caddies are packed with every imaginable type of tea, fine china graces the tea trays, and the bathrooms are supplied with every extra. Five hot courses are always available for dinner if reservations are made in advance. There are enough activities nearby to occupy a week and the Jeffersons have maps marked for exploration of the Elgar Trail, the Potteries, Shakespeare country, and the Cotswolds. *Directions:* Upton Snodsbury is located 6 miles east of Worcester on the A422. Turn right by the Red Lion on the B4082 towards Pershore and Upton House is by the church.

UPTON HOUSE
Owners Angela & Hugh Jefferson
Upton Snodsbury
Worcester, Worcestershire WR7 4NR
Tel: (090560) 226
3 rooms with private bathrooms
From £30 per person
Closed Christmas
No children
Wolsey Lodge

Acres of glorious gardens have been meticulously laid out by Tulip Bemrose: garden design is one of this energetic lady's many interests. When I visited The Old Rectory I found Tulip in her rose garden busily dead-heading the roses. The air was heavy with the scent of flowers as we walked through her "wild" garden, into the walled garden, and onto the paved terrace where the air was buzzing with the sound of bees feeding on the banks of lavender. Stepping through the French windows into the drawing room, I found that Tulip has decorated her house in the same pleasing way that she has designed her garden, artfully displaying her lovely antique furniture and selecting fabrics that complement this beautifully proportioned house. She dines with her guests around the large dining room table and encourages them to bring their own wine to accompany her cooking. The three very large bedrooms are spacious and each has a very large bathroom. The master bedroom has an adjacent small single bedroom. There is a lot to see and do in the area: the rugged Yorkshire Dales lie close at hand as does Fountains Abbey. The walled city of York is less than an hour's drive away. *Directions:* Travel north on the A1 and take the A61 towards Ripon. After 1 mile turn right at the signpost for Melmerby and Wath. The house is the first on the left opposite the church behind a high stone wall.

THE OLD RECTORY
Owner Tulip Bemrose
Wath
Ripon, Yorkshire HG4 5ET
Tel: (0765) 84311
3 rooms with private bathrooms
From £30 per person
Closed Christmas
Children over 7
Wolsey Lodge

This is a large old family farmhouse with stables to one side, a swimming pool behind, and acres of lawns with mature trees and shrubbery that sweep down to an old moat and Elizabeth Olesen is the epitome of an old-fashioned farmer's wife. While guests may use the large elegant drawing room with its views across the lawns, they usually prefer to gather in the snug parlor, warmed on chilly evenings by a cheerful blaze in the pretty, carved-pine fireplace. Breakfast is the only meal served at the long, polished dining-room table. The two high-ceilinged, old-fashioned bedrooms have their own bathrooms and the small nursery room is usually occupied by children. Red and blue horse-drawn gypsy caravans decorate the stable yard, all equipped and available for leisurely explorations of the surrounding countryside. West Lexham is a tiny rural village consisting of simply The Hall and a few cottages, several of which are available for weekly rental. It is centrally placed for enjoying Norfolk's many sights such as the great houses of Felbrigg, Blickling, and Houghton, the Royal Family's home, Sandringham, and a great many private gardens open on summer weekends. Norfolk's capital Norwich has a magnificent Norman cathedral and castle museum. *Directions:* From the south, leave the M11 at exit 9 and take the A11 to Barton Mills (bypass Newmarket on the A45), then the A1065 towards Swaffham. West Lexham is midway between Swaffham and Fakenham immediately to the east of the A1065.

THE HALL
Owner Elizabeth Olesen
West Lexham
King's Lynn, Norfolk PE32 2QN
Tel: (0760) 755244
3 rooms, 2 with private bathrooms
From £21 per person
Closed Christmas
Children welcome

The Old Chapel bed and breakfast, a former place of worship, sits in the heart of the rugged Derbyshire village of Wetton. The comfy lounge at the top of a short flight of stairs has a lofty ceiling rising high above to the chapel rafters and is furnished with low tables and large plump cushions arranged on the floor for seating. The adjacent dining area has cafe-style chairs and small round tables arranged in intimate groupings, and is a cozy spot to enjoy the full English breakfast served here. Hostess Dana Sera, originally from Italy, prepares dinners by reservation, usually featuring Italian, French, Chinese, or Indian cuisine. The bedrooms are found on the ground floor and have simple, pretty decor; a great many with Laura Ashley bed linen, curtains, and wallpaper, but none have a view. For sightseeing, besides walking in the Derbyshire Dales (Manifold Valley, Milldale, and Dovedale), guests can visit the potteries (Spode and Wedgwood, for example), stately homes (Chatsworth House and Haddon Hall), gardens, and picturesque villages (Hartington, Tissington, and Ilam), all within easy driving distance. *Directions:* From Ashbourne follow the A515, signposted Buxton, for 6 miles to The New Inns. Take the left turn signposted Milldale and Alstonfield. Descend the hill, cross the river, and fork left to Milldale, following the river to the Watts Russell Arms. Turn left just past the pub and follow this road into Wetton. Take the road opposite the Royal Oak pub, and The Old Chapel is on the left.

THE OLD CHAPEL
Owners Dana & Sere Sera
Wetton
Ashbourne, Derbyshire DE6 2AF
Tel: (033527) 378
5 rooms, 4 with private bathrooms
From £25 per person
Closed Christmas
Children over 7

When Rosalie and Ian Buckle first moved to Dunsley Hall, once a wealthy shipping family's grand holiday home, it was in a badly neglected state. The Buckles set to work exposing the oak floor, refurbishing the golden oak paneling, adding modern bathrooms, and turning part of the hall into four self-catering units. Then they relandscaped the gardens, tidied up the tennis courts, and built a spectacular heated pool and fitness room. The *piece de resistance* of this lovely home is the large billiard room which has golden oak-paneled walls, a massive carved fireplace with built-in seats, and beautiful stained glass windows depicting squareriggers sailing on an aqua sea beneath a cloud-dappled sky. The paneled lounge is snug and cozy with its old-fashioned fireplace and soft carpet. The bedrooms are beautifully decorated in pastel-colored wallpapers with coordinating drapes framing the stone-mullioned windows. A large downstairs corner room has a romantic brass four-poster bed. The nearby North Yorkshire moors with their picturesque villages snuggled into sheltered valleys are a great draw for visitors as are the quaint fishing villages of Runswick Bay, Staithes, and Robin Hood's Bay. *Directions:* From York take the A64 to the A169 Pickering/Whitby road. Cross the moors through Sleights to the A171. Turn left (away from Whitby) and first right to Dunsley. The Hall is in the village on the right.

DUNSLEY HALL
Owners Rosalie & Ian Buckle
Dunsley
Whitby, Yorkshire YO21 3TL
Tel: (0947) 83437
5 rooms with private bathrooms
From £28 per person
Closed Christmas
Credit cards all major
Children welcome

In the Lake District it seems that "run-of-the-mill" hotels and guesthouses are a dime a dozen, so I was thrilled when I found an exceptional one in The Archway Guest House in the center of Windermere village. Hosts Aurea and Tony Greenhalgh serve mouthwatering breakfasts which offer homemade yogurt sweetened with a dash of honey and topped with fruit puree, American pancakes with syrup, and apple griddle cakes with butter and syrup as well as a traditional farmhouse breakfast. The Greenhalghs pride themselves on serving homemade foods, using organic ingredients whenever possible. Dinners are fresh and delicious and are accompanied by a choice of six red and six white wines. All the rooms are decorated in keeping with a Victorian home, from country pine in the dining room to antique quilts gracing the beds. The bedrooms and bathrooms are small, even tiny, but are very well equipped. The Archway is located in the heart of the Lake District, an area known for its outstanding beauty. An information book in every bedroom lists walks in the area for which Tony supplies maps. More leisurely exercise can be obtained by strolling into town on a shopping excursion. *Directions:* Exit the M6 at junction 36 and take the A591 around Kendal towards Ambleside. Shortly after passing Windermere's train station, turn left on Elleray Road and right into College Road. The Archway is on the left.

THE ARCHWAY GUEST HOUSE
Owners Aurea & Tony Greenhalgh
13 College Road
Windermere, Cumbria LA23 1BY
Tel: (09662) 5613
6 rooms with private bathrooms
From £21 per person
Open all year
Children over 12
No Smoking house

Hawksmoor Guest House appears no different from the many other guesthouses on these well-travelled Lake District roads until one enters, sees, and appreciates the "apple-pie-order" of Robert and Barbara Tyson's home. The decor is not fancy or pretentious, for this is not an expensive country house hotel, but it is well maintained; Robert boasts, "If it's broken or damaged today, it will be fixed tomorrow." The dining room is delightfully set with pink tablecloths covered with delicate lace and laid with silver service. Barbara is happy for guests to eat in or out, always willing to provide a traditional English three-course dinner of an appetizer, roast with three vegetables, and a dessert such as apple pie and custard. Guests have a small comfortable lounge at their disposal. The bedrooms are smallish but each is decorated with pretty flowered wallpaper, matching curtains and bedspreads, and all have an ensuite bathroom. Robert is an expert on the Lake District and even manages to suggest a sight or two to the hurried traveller who is dashing through this lovely part of England and using it as a one-night stop on the road between London and Edinburgh. He has found that these rushed travellers often return for a stay of several days. Windermere is in the heart of the busy southern Lake District, easily accessible from the M6. *Directions:* Windermere is just off the A591 Ambleside to Kendal road. Drive along New Road and look for Hawksmoor on the right just after the clock tower.

HAWKSMOOR GUEST HOUSE
Owners Barbara & Robert Tyson
Lake Road
Windermere, Cumbria LA23 2EQ
Tel: (09662) 2110
10 rooms with private bathrooms
From £25 per person
Closed December
Children over 6

The Old Wharf's idyllic setting provides an entrancing first impression. A lane leading off the main highway wends its way down to a delightful small inn hugging the edge of a tiny canal where in summer swans swim gracefully among the reeds. Nearby, cows graze peacefully in meadows which stretch as far as the eye can see. The enclosed front patio is ablaze with a riot of color: an English garden of splendid flowers, beautifully manicured yet artfully exuberant. The side of the house that opens onto the meandering stream is laced with climbing pink roses. The spell of the initial impression remains unbroken when you go inside. Moira and David have taken an old warehouse and converted it into an outstanding small bed and breakfast. The decor throughout is fresh and airy and extremely pretty, with nothing contrived or stuffy. Moira has managed to cleverly combine lovely pastel fabrics with natural wood-finish antiques to achieve a very sophisticated country look. Although David is busy farming he also helps Moira and both offer guests a sincerely warm welcome. Breakfast is the only meal served. Within easy reach are the towns of the Sussex coast, Petworth House, and Arundel Castle. *Directions:* From Billingshurst take the A272 towards Petworth, cross the canal and river, and the drive to The Old Wharf is 50 yards after the river on the left.

THE OLD WHARF
Owners Moira & David Mitchell
Wisborough Green
Billingshurst, Sussex RH14 OJG
Tel: (0403) 784096
4 rooms with private baths
From £25 to £35 per person
Closed Christmas
Credit cards all major
Children over 12
No Smoking house

18 St Paul's Square is one of several large Victorian terrace homes which border a grassy square down one of York's quiet side streets. From the outside, it looks just like many other houses in this "up and coming" neighborhood, but inside it is delightfully different, showcasing colorful "country Victorian" decor by Ann and Mike Beaufoy. A sunny yellow hallway rises from the entry, setting the cheerful mood felt throughout the house. In the sitting room sage green leafy wallpaper serves as a backdrop for an old country dresser displaying blue and white willow dishes and an old gray marble fireplace looking much as it must have done in Victorian times. Three of the bedrooms are spacious and airy, and the fourth is a small single room. I particularly admired the double room with the brass and iron bedstead covered with a patchwork bedspread and warm pine furniture. For sightseeing, after you have exhausted the many possibilities in York, there are excursions to the North York Moors and the Dales, and tours of stately homes (Castle Howard is a must) and ecclesiastical ruins (Rievaulx and Fountains Abbey). *Directions:* Leave the A64 (which forms the southern part of the York Outer Ring Road) at the A1036 in the direction of York city center. Pass the racecourse and as the walls of York come into view turn left on Holgate Road (A59 Harrogate). After crossing the railway tracks look for a right turn to St Paul's Square.

18 ST PAUL'S SQUARE
Owners Ann & Mike Beaufoy
18 St Paul's Square
York Y02 4BD
Tel: (0904) 629884
4 rooms with private bathrooms
From £25 per person
Closed Christmas
Children welcome
Wolsey Lodge

Just a few yards from York's city walls, South Parade is a private cobbled street adjacent to a very busy main road. Inside Number 4 is a world of quiet repose, where you are invited to partake of tea and hot buttered scones in the elegant drawing room. Bedrooms are all furnished to the highest standards; bathrooms are sparkling and have powerful showers, brass fittings, and are well equipped with many "extras." All the rooms are decorated in soft pastels; one in soft blue-grays, another in shades of peach with matching bedspreads and drapes coordinating with the wall covering. On the top floor, a larger suite with a sitting area and writing desk gives guests lots of room for relaxation should they prefer the privacy of their room to the drawing room. With advance notice Ann is happy to provide either a light supper or a four-course dinner, and meals are taken in the below-stairs room that was once the kitchen. Ann and Robin are mines of information on York and the surrounding countryside and they really put themselves out to steer visitors in the right direction. Guests often enjoy a bus tour of the Dales and Moors. *Directions:* Leave the A64 (which forms the southern part of the York Outer Ring Road) at the A1036, in the direction of York city center, following signs for the racecourse. Pass the racecourse, and as you see the Odeon Cinema on the left turn right into a narrow street (next to a car showroom) which is South Parade.

4 SOUTH PARADE
Owners Ann & Robin McClure
4 South Parade
York YO2 2BA
Tel: (0904) 628229
3 rooms, 2 with private bathrooms
From £31 per person
Closed Christmas
No children
No Smoking house

At one time Fulford was a village separated from the walled city of York by miles of green fields, but over the years York has expanded and today one cannot distinguish where Fulford ends and York begins. The Dower House peeps over a tall hedge on the corner of Fulford's main street (the A19 to York) and wide gates open to admit guests and their cars to the grounds. Inside this 200-year-old house the entry, dining room, and large living room have warm, golden pine woodwork and are traditionally furnished with antiques, soft, pleasing color schemes, and a crackling log fire in the stone fireplace. The most interesting of the bedrooms has an artfully draped half-tester pine bed, ensuite bathroom, and an adjoining tiny single room, making it perfect for families. A two-night Yuletide holiday offers carol service in the Minster, a visit to York's pantomime, and traditional Christmas fare at table. Diana provides maps and outlines directions for exploring. Because parking in York is a problem, guests usually board the local bus for the 2-mile journey into the city. It takes several days to explore The Minster, The Treasurer's House, Jorvik Viking Centre, Clifford's tower, York Castle Museum, and the National Railway Museum. *Directions:* Leave the A64 (which forms the southern part of the York Outer Ring Road) at the A19, in the direction of York city center. The Dower House is on the right just after you enter Fulford.

THE DOWER HOUSE
Owner Diana Calder
Fulford
York YO1 4PP
Tel: (0904) 633508
3 rooms, 2 with private bathrooms
From £25 per person
Open all year
Children over 12
Wolsey Lodge

Places that Welcome Children

(no age limit)

No Smoking Houses

Bath, Somerset House, 24
Boltongate, The Old Rectory, 29
Bosham, Hatpins, 30
Bovey Tracey, Willmead Farm, 33
Bradford on Avon, Bradford Old Windmill, 34
Bradford on Avon - Avoncliff, Weavers Mill, 36
Brithem Bottom, Lower Beers, 37
Broadway, Cowley House, 39
Castle Hedingham, The Old Schoolhouse, 46
Crediton, The Thatched Cottage, 55
Dursley - Stinchcombe, Drakeston House, 57
Hartfield, Bolebroke Mill, 66
Little Rissington, Little Rissington Manor, 82
Longdon, The Moat House, 84
Morchard Bishop, Wigham, 90
Penryn, Bella's Mouse, 98
Rogate, Mizzards Farm, 101
Ruan High Lanes - Treworga, Treworga Farmhouse, 104
Salisbury, Stratford Lodge, 109
Speen, Speen Cottage, 114
St Blazey, Nanscawen, 116
Stogumber, Curdon Mill, 121
Windermere, The Archway Guest House, 133
Wisborough Green, The Old Wharf, 135
York, 4 South Parade, 137

Members of Wolsey Lodges

Index

INN DISCOVERIES FROM OUR READERS

Some editions of *KAREN BROWN'S COUNTRY INN GUIDES* include a list of hotels recommended by our readers. We have received many letters describing wonderful inns you have discovered; however, we have never included them until we had the opportunity to make a personal inspection. This seemed a waste of some marvelous "tips". Therefore, in order to feature them we have added a section called "Inn Discoveries from Our Readers".

If you have a favorite discovery you would be willing to share with other travellers who love to travel the "inn way", please let us hear from you and include the following information:

1. *Your name, address and telephone number.*

2. *Name, address and telephone number of "your inn".*

3. *Brochure or picture of inn (we cannot return material).*

4. *Written permission to use an edited version of your description.*

5. *Would you want your name, city and state included in the book?*

In addition to our current guide books, we are also researching future books in Europe and updating those previously published. We would appreciate comments on any of your favorites. The types of inns we would love to hear about are those with special old-world ambiance, charm and atmosphere. We need a brochure or picture so that we can select those which most closely follow the mood of our guides. We look forward to hearing from you. Thank you.

Karen Brown's Country Inn Guides, Post Office Box 70, San Mateo, CA 94401
Telephone (415) 342-9117 Fax (415) 342-9153

English, Welsh & Scottish Country Inns

10 Regional Driving Itineraries
London Sightseeing & Hotels
British Country House Hotels

English Country Bed & Breakfasts is the companion guide to ***English, Welsh & Scottish Country Inns*** which has four sections: practical information useful in planning your trip; driving itineraries (throughout England, Scotland, and Wales) where charming hotel accommodation is linked with sightseeing suggestions; London hotels and sightseeing; and a listing of outstanding places to stay in England, Scotland, and Wales.

The ten driving itineraries explore a particular region's scenic beauty, history, and culture and suggest a hotel for each night's stay. If the hotel we suggest is not for you, you can enjoy the holiday by following our sightseeing routes and using accommodation suggestions from ***English Country Bed & Breakfasts.*** We use the term "inns" to mean charming establishments that we recommend, places that are our favorites, preferably owned and run by an attentive family.

Karen Brown's Country Inn Guides

The Essential Travel Companion

Regional itineraries guide you through the countryside and suggest a charming inn for each nights stay. The Places to Stay section includes a selective listing of dramatic castles, cozy chalets, historic manors, romantic villas and much more – all personally inspected and honestly described.

Order Form

KAREN BROWN'S COUNTRY INN GUIDES

Please ask in your local bookstore for KAREN BROWN'S COUNTRY INN guides. If the books you want are unavailable, you may order directly from the publisher.

AUSTRIAN COUNTRY INNS & CASTLES $12.95

CALIFORNIA COUNTRY INNS & ITINERARIES $12.95

ENGLISH COUNTRY BED & BREAKFASTS $12.95

ENGLISH, WELSH & SCOTTISH COUNTRY INNS $12.95

EUROPEAN COUNTRY CUISINE - ROMANTIC INNS & RECIPES $10.95

FRENCH COUNTRY BED & BREAKFASTS $12.95

FRENCH COUNTRY INNS & CHÂTEAUX $12.95

GERMAN COUNTRY INNS & CASTLES $12.95

IRISH COUNTRY INNS $12.95

ITALIAN COUNTRY INNS & VILLAS $12.95

PORTUGUESE COUNTRY INNS & POUSADAS $12.95

SCANDINAVIAN COUNTRY INNS & MANORS $12.95

SPANISH COUNTRY INNS & PARADORS $12.95

SWISS COUNTRY INNS & CHALETS $12.95

Name ______________________ *Street* ____________________

City ______________________ *State* _____ *Zip* __________

Add $2.50 for the first book and .50 for each additional book for postage & packing.
California residents add 7% sales tax.
Indicate the number of copies of each title. Send in form with your check to:

KAREN BROWN'S COUNTRY INN GUIDES
Post Office Box 70
San Mateo, California 94401
Tel: (415) 342-9117 Fax: (415) 342-9153

KAREN BROWN wrote her first travel guide, *French Country Inns & Chateaux*, in 1979. Now there are 14 books in the Karen Brown series which offers the most personalized, reliable guides describing charming lodging from grand castles to cozy farmhouses. Karen lives at Seal Cove Inn, in Moss Beach, California with her husband, Rick, and their children, Alexandra and Richard.

CLARE BROWN has specialized in planning European countryside itineraries for many years. Now her expertise is available to a much larger audience--the readers of her daughter Karen's guides. Clare lives in the San Francisco Bay area with her husband, Bill. Their son, Bill, and his wife, Heidi, live nearby with their three children. Another daughter, Kimberly, is studying hotel management in Colorado.

JUNE BROWN, born and raised in Sheffield, England now lives in San Mateo, California with her husband, Tony, son Simon, and daughter Clare. Over the last seven years June has undertaken extensive research trips to Germany, Ireland, and her mother country for the Karen Brown guidebooks.

BARBARA TAPP is the talented professional artist responsible for the pen and ink drawings in *English Country Bed & Breakfasts.* Born and raised in Sydney, Australia, Barbara now lives in the San Francisco Bay area with her husband, Richard, their sons, Jonathan and Alexander, and their daughter, Georgia.

CHRISTINA LADAS, who painted the cover painting, was born and raised in the New York City area where she still resides with her friend and helper, daughter Erena. Christina's mother, interior designer Zoe Ladas, encouraged her daughter's artistic abilities from an early age, which contributes to her success today as an artist whose wide range of talent leads her into almost every field of art.